# Human
## Trafficking &
## Modern Slavery

Introducing the issue and recognising the signs

Mike Emberson

Published by The Medaille Trust
Cathedral Centre
3 Ford Street
Salford
M3 6DP
Tel: 0161 817 2260
E-mail: www.medaille-trust.org.uk    enquiries@medaille-trust.org.uk

A registered charity limited by guarantee
Registered Charity Number: 1117830
Copyright © The Medaille Trust 2018

First published February 2019

ISBN 9780852314852

### Dedication

This book is dedicated to all those victims of human trafficking and modern slavery who still wait to be rescued, to Sister Ann Teresa of the Order of St Joseph of Annecy and the staff of the Medaille Trust.

### Acknowledgements

Many people have worked hard to make this book possible. The author would particularly like to thank Sharon Benning-Prince for her significant help and guidance with regards to several chapters, and to also thank the following for their valuable contributions and assistance which are gratefully acknowledged:

Jonathan Blagbrough
Sr Janet Fearns
Charlotte Grainger
Garry Smith

The Medaille Trust
Redemptorist Publications

In order to illustrate some points made in this book a variety of case studies have been used. For security and confidentiality reasons all real names have been changed.

Printed by 4edge Limited, Essex SS5 4AD

# CONTENTS

# INTRODUCTION

Human trafficking and slavery. How often do you think about these issues? Is it just when the television news shows yet another police raid on a camp or some building, taking away several people, some in handcuffs and others wrapped in blankets?

Perhaps "trafficking" is something which, in your mind, is related to perilous migrant journeys across the Mediterranean in unseaworthy boats? When rescuers pull people from turbulent waters, national and international discussions are inconclusive and frustratingly similar.

What about slavery? Isn't that something that happened in the past? Surely there must be "rules" about such things?

Would you be surprised to know that people are regularly bought and sold on Oxford Street in central London?

News reports suggest that trafficking and slavery are here, in our midst, in the UK. How might they be recognised? Is there something we can do to stop it?

That's what this book is about.

# THE MEDAILLE TRUST

The indefatigable Sr Eugenia Bonetti, an Italian Consolata Missionary with many years of missionary experience in Africa, repeatedly met African women on the streets of Rome. They told her their stories of being trafficked and forced to work as prostitutes or as domestic servants, pleading for somewhere safe to stay where they might start to rebuild their lives. "We have safe houses", she declared. "We have plenty of safe houses. We have convents!" With that flash of inspiration, a network involving more than seventy religious Congregations and several hundred Sisters in thirty countries came to birth.

"The network is everything", Sr Eugenia explained. "It is a network that goes beyond the boundaries of Italy and involves some thirty countries of origin, transit and destination of trafficked girls. Everywhere, local sisters are carrying on the precious work of prevention and rehabilitation, of protection of girls and their families, of welcoming those who are repatriated. It means that if a woman presents herself in one place, we can move her somewhere safer."

This amazing work done by so many Religious across the world receives no publicity when the media speaks of efforts to combat people-trafficking. In one way, that is good. Drawing too much attention to the existence of a line of convents offering safe havens could be risky. Yet, at the same time, it is good for the world to know that Sisters are at the frontline of the battle against one of the world's most tragic problems.

The Medaille Trust fits into this scenario. The UK-based organisation was founded by Religious Congregations in 2006. Its primary mission "is the empowerment of women, men and children, who have been freed from the human-trafficking and the modern day slavery industry in the UK, enabling them to regain their dignity and self-worth. We do this by providing safe housing and offering opportunities for physical and psychological healing, rehabilitation and protection to the victims in our care." (http://www.medaille-trust.org.uk/what-we-do/victim-care)

The Medaille Trust, arguably one of the first to enter the UK field and the largest Catholic charity currently engaged in anti-trafficking work, currently has five dedicated women's houses, three male houses and one specialist family centre, offering up to 109 bed spaces at any one time to women, men and children.

# ST JOSEPHINE BAKHITA, THE PATRON SAINT OF SLAVES

"If I were to meet the slave-traders who kidnapped me and even those who tortured me, I would kneel and kiss their hands, for if that did not happen, I would not be a Christian and Religious today... The Lord has loved me so much: we must love everyone... we must be compassionate!"

*St Josephine Bakhita*

The patron saint of slaves is St Josephine Bakhita, captured at about the age of nine in her native Sudan. The slavers gave her the name "Bakhita", which means "lucky" or "fortunate".

Yet Bakhita's is no story from ancient times. Born in Darfur in approximately 1869, she was sold five times and finally given away. She suffered appalling cruelty at the hands of her owners – so much so that she even forgot her name – but the tragedy is that her treatment was probably fairly typical of the time. She herself related the following incident:

"One day I unwittingly made a mistake that incensed the master's son. He became furious, snatched me violently from my hiding place, and began to strike me ferociously with the lash and his feet. Finally he left me half dead, completely unconscious. Some slaves carried me away and lay me on a straw mat, where I remained for over a month. A woman skilled in this cruel art [tattooing] came to the general's house... our mistress stood behind us, whip in hand. The woman had a dish of white flour, a dish of salt and a razor. When she had made her patterns, the woman took the razor and made incisions along the lines. Salt was poured into each of the wounds. My face was spared, but six patterns were designed on my breasts, and sixty more on my belly and arms. I thought I would die, especially when salt was poured in the wounds... it was by a miracle of God I didn't die. He had destined me for better things."

Bakhita's final owners were an Italian family from whom she finally escaped, thanks to the Canossian Sisters in Venice. Amazingly, an Italian court ruled in 1889 that, because Sudan had outlawed slavery before Bakhita was born and because Italy did not recognise slavery, she had never legally been a slave!

When captured as a child, Bakhita was forced to become a Muslim. Freed, she chose to become a Catholic and, in 1893, entered with the Canossian Sisters who had saved her. When Bakhita died on 8 February 1947, thousands of people paid their respects to the former slave, whom Pope St John Paul II canonised on 1 October 2000.

# CHAPTER ONE

## What are human trafficking and modern slavery?

### Setting the scene

"I thought I was coming to this country to work as a hairdresser. The man who accompanied me offered to look after my passport when we landed at the airport. He said it would leave me free to look after my luggage. We drove to the 'hotel' – only it wasn't a hotel. It was a dirty, cramped room at the top of an old building. He refused to return my passport and said that I would have to work to pay back the cost of my air ticket."

*Chamba*

## Chiefs have slaves

"Imagine yourself in a busy market. Somebody tells you, in an offhand manner, 'Those three men beside you are slaves' and continues examining a mound of vegetables on the market stall. Evidently slaves are a fact of life, to be readily dismissed without further enquiry. The three men, identically dressed in a durable, inexpensive material of an off-white colour, were also buying vegetables. 'They probably belong to the local chief', I was told. 'Chiefs have slaves.'"

*Sr Janet*

This might sound a strange question, but, here in Britain, have you ever met someone who is a slave? How do you know whether you have or have not? The frightening thing is that, in today's society, there is no particular way of identifying a slave just by their appearance. There is no immediate way of knowing that a young nanny, sitting on a bench and watching the children, has had her passport confiscated, is threatened with dire consequences to her family should she try to escape and is working an eighteen-hour day, six or seven days of the week, for little or no pay. How can you know that her slender figure is the result of hunger rather than frequent visits to the local gym?

As you walk down London's Oxford Street, is it obvious that a small group of people, apparently enjoying a conversation, is actually selling one of them, perhaps into prostitution, perhaps into domestic slavery? That is the problem which faces the police and social services, the Church and others who would try to rescue and protect the victims. How can they rescue invisible people?

Many countries where slavery has been technically abolished have memorials to the countless men, women and children whom others sold or perhaps tricked, captured or even just handed over into servitude. Liverpool children have long heard of the dark side of their Industrial Revolution history, when the city thrived on cotton and other goods purchased in exchange for human lives. Today its International Slavery Museum tells the dreadful story in unforgettable detail... but today's victims of the modern slave trade need action now.

Human trafficking and modern slavery represent two of the great evils prevalent in the world today. These evils can touch and irreparably damage the lives of people from any country, of any age, gender, background or circumstance.

Some individuals, or groups, because of their vulnerability, are more at risk than others. Many are drawn by the prospect of well-paid work and future security.

Those who are already discriminated against on the basis of caste, lifestyle, ethnicity or gender are more likely than others to become the prey of unscrupulous traffickers.

Environments where there is conflict or social unrest, the rule of law is weak or corruption is rife represent fertile breeding grounds for this trade in human lives.

## The historical context

"From time immemorial, different societies have known the phenomenon of man's subjugation by man. There have been periods of human history in which the institution of slavery was generally accepted and regulated by law. This legislation dictated who was born free and who was born into slavery, as well as the conditions whereby a freeborn person could lose his or her freedom or regain it. In other words, the law itself admitted that some people were able, or required, to be considered the property of other people, at their free disposition. A slave could be bought and sold, given away or acquired, as if he or she were a commercial product.

Today, as the result of a growth in our awareness, slavery, seen as a crime against humanity, has been formally abolished throughout the world. The right of each person not to be kept in a state of slavery or servitude has been recognized in international law as inviolable.

Yet, even though the international community has adopted numerous agreements aimed at ending slavery in all its forms, and has launched various strategies to combat this phenomenon, millions of people today – children, women and men of all ages – are deprived of freedom and are forced to live in conditions akin to slavery."

*Pope Francis, Message for the World Day of Peace, 1 January 2015*

A tree stands on the roadside through the town of Kabwe, Zambia, a long-established centre for trade – and that is the heart-breaking history of that tree.

Today, the tree is surrounded by a small fence, marked with a simple sign, "Slave Tree". In days gone by, this was where Arab traders purchased their human supplies, sometimes brought along by their own people, sometimes captured whilst going about their ordinary daily lives. Kabwe, or Broken Hill as it was known, had a thriving slave market. The tree was a convenient landmark, its shade helping to keep the traders comfortable and the slaves in a better condition than if they had been forced to stand in the sun.

Was Elizabeth Mwanza's grandmother brought to Kabwe? Elizabeth was an excellent midwife and married to a secondary school teacher approximately five hundred miles from Kabwe. "Grandmother" is a somewhat generic term for a female ancestor within the space of a few generations and so Elizabeth did not know what year it was when the Arab traders passed by the village. "My grandmother and her sister were small children. They saw some strange men and were curious. When the men offered them a piece of the chicken they were cooking, my grandmother accepted but her sister did not trust them. She ran home to tell her father. He and the other men in the village picked up their spears and went to investigate, but when they reached the clearing, the strange men and my grandmother had disappeared. She was never seen again. The men were slave traders."

Travel further north towards the magnificent Lake Mweru and Kashikishi, and it is impossible to miss a single row of palm trees on the skyline. These are also slave trees. These mark the place where traders made their captives sit and eat before continuing their journey. The trees sprang up from the discarded coconuts, but they form an unforgettable memorial to tragedy.

Arguably, slavery in one form or another has existed since early humans first began to form the organised groups that we have now termed societies.

Most people are familiar with the concept of slavery and its practices. They might, if asked, give the examples of the Roman Empire or the American South before the Civil War. However, slavery in all its forms has existed down the centuries and across many forms of society. It has often been racial and gender-biased, state-sponsored and spread by colonialism.

## Chattel slavery

For most people the starting point for understanding slavery is the familiar concept of chattel slavery.

A very familiar example of this type of slavery was the Atlantic slave trade from Africa to the Americas during the period of the sixteenth to nineteenth centuries. It is called chattel slavery because individual human beings are treated as property or "chattels" of their purchaser or owner and are bought and sold as goods or, in quantity, as a commodity.

Under most chattel slavery systems the children of the slaves involved inherited, at birth, the enslaved status of their parents. It was the dominant form of slavery, and arguably in some cases, the dominant structure of society, for thousands of years until recently when, at various times, it was abolished.

No legal system of any country currently permits or condones chattel slavery in any form. It continues to exist, however, in rare pockets throughout the world and is, in some instances, such as Mauritania, the beneficiary of state tolerance or indifference.

## Has slavery ended?

"What could I do? My husband had abandoned me, leaving me with three young children. I tried hard to find work. I begged. I sold almost everything I had. In the end, all I had left to feed my children was my own body. I hated it. I hated myself, but we had food."

*Bwalya*

"I had no choice. At first I refused to work as a prostitute but my 'owner' refused to give me food until, when I was starving, I gave in and accepted a client. My 'owner' told me that he knew my village and had friends who would kill my parents if ever again I refused to please his clients."

*Chipya*

Question: Not all prostitutes have made a lifestyle choice. Sometimes they must either "work the streets" or cause their families to suffer. What would you do in such circumstances?

In September 2011, the UK media buzzed with the news that twenty-four men had been held in captivity at the Greenacres travellers' site in Leighton Buzzard, Bedfordshire. A senior police officer explained:

> The men we found at the site were in a poor state of physical health and the conditions they were living in were shockingly filthy and cramped. We believe that some of them had been living and working there in a state of virtual slavery, some for just a few weeks and others for up to fifteen years.

He explained that their captors had targeted vulnerable people:

> They're recruited and told if you come here we'll pay you £80 a day; we'll look after you, give you board and lodgings. But when they get here, their hair is cut off them, they're kept in some cases [in] horseboxes, dog kennels and old caravans, made to work for no money, given very, very small amounts of food. That's the worst case. Some are treated a little bit better, but they are told they could not leave and if they did they will be beaten up and attacked.

Many of us are familiar with the inspiring stories of the white abolitionists of the UK, figures such as Thomas Clarkson, William Wilberforce and Granville Sharp. Some of us may also know the names of key black figures in the fight against slavery: Mary Prince, Ottobah Cugoano, Olaudah Equiano, Ukawsaw Gronniosaw and Louis Celeste Lecesne.

Unfortunately, their work was never completed. Slavery did not end with abolition in the nineteenth century. Modern slavery still blights our society and harms people all over the world.

Slavery continues today in every country in the world: women forced into prostitution; people forced to work in agriculture, domestic work and factories; children in sweatshops produce goods to be sold globally; entire families forced to work for nothing to pay off generational debts; forced marriage...

Definitions of trafficking and slavery may have changed over time, and indeed the nature of slavery, in many instances, has changed, but it is still with us.

## The contemporary context

In general terms, the contemporary exploitation of human beings may be divided into human trafficking and modern slavery.

> "Today, as in the past, slavery is rooted in a notion of the human person which allows him or her to be treated as an object. Whenever sin corrupts the human heart and distances us from our Creator and our neighbours, the latter are no longer regarded as beings of equal dignity, as brothers or sisters sharing a common humanity, but rather as objects. Whether by coercion or deception, or by physical or psychological duress, human persons created in the image and likeness of God are deprived of their freedom, sold and reduced to being the property of others. They are treated as a means to an end."
>
> *Pope Francis, Message for the World Day of Peace, 1 January 2015*

Modern slavery is hard to define, its understanding largely based on a human rights approach.

The concept of human rights has deep roots in history. Documents like (arguably) the Magna Carta in 1215 or the American Declaration of Independence in 1776 laid down some of the building blocks for our current understanding.

The horror and ensuing chaos of the Second World War made the clarification, protection and enforcing of human rights a priority. The creation of the United Nations provided the necessary vehicle to drive things forward.

Fifty member states contributed to the final draft of the Universal Declaration of Human Rights, adopted in 1948. This was the first attempt to set out, at a global level, the fundamental rights and freedoms to be shared by all people "of every tribe and tongue and people and nation" (Revelation 7:9).

The Declaration forms the basis of the European Convention on Human Rights, adopted in 1950 with UK lawyers and Sir Winston Churchill playing a key role in its drafting. The UK's Human Rights Act of 1998 made these rights part of UK domestic law.

Article 4 of that Act outlaws slavery, stating that:

- No one shall be held in slavery or servitude.
- No one shall be required to perform forced or compulsory labour.

However, this and many other documents often fail to define exactly what slavery actually is.

Article 4 also uses the term "forced labour" which is again ill-defined. Perhaps this lack of clarity has led us to ignore, until recently, modern forms of slavery.

Arguably the most helpful remark that has been made on the subject is "you know it when you see it".

## Indenture

- You want to borrow some money and you agree to work off your debt.
- You want to take up the offer of an apprenticeship and so you agree to work for a fixed length of time, perhaps at a lower rate of pay, in exchange for your training.
- Question: have you freely agreed to a clearly-defined job description and a fixed length of time?

Indenture as slavery takes on a variety of forms including bonded labour and debt bondage.

The services required in order to redeem the debt and their duration

- may be badly or ill defined
- may be passed from generation to generation, with children required to pay off their parents' debt
- constitute the current, most widespread, form of slavery
- encourage people to borrow money and to lose control of both their employment conditions and the debt itself

## Forced labour

You are working against your will because, if you don't, your employer threatens to hurt you or a member of your family. Someone else controls the what, when, how, and length of time that you work. You are not free to "lay down tools" and walk away – even for such simple things as a cup of coffee, a lunch break or to go to the toilet.

Someone in these circumstances may be said to be in slavery if any or all of the following are present:

- They are forced to work, possibly under physical, mental or emotional threat
- They are owned or controlled by an employer
- They are de-humanised, treated as a commodity or bought and sold as property
- They are physically constrained or have restrictions placed on their freedom of movement
- They are a child who is forced to work. (Child slavery is often confused with child labour. Child labour is harmful for children and hinders their education and development but may in some contexts be understandable. Child slavery occurs when a child's labour is exploited for someone else's gain.)

Those in most urgent need of help are repeatedly too frightened to leave their "employers", warned of dire consequences to their families should they try to escape. Frequently they are told that if they go to the police, they will be immediately deported. Once again this is a lie to keep them in captivity. More often than we know, a woman is locked in the house where she is forced to work, with no means of escape and perhaps no language to communicate should she manage to leave her enslavement. Physical violence is a common weapon, rendering her too afraid to risk yet another beating.

## Other forms of slavery

Forms of forced and indentured labour vary and whilst it is useful to think of brick kilns in India, cobalt mines in Africa or agricultural workers in the Americas as good examples of the phenomenon, we must be conscious that slavery can and does exist in any setting that is based on commercial activity which is trading goods or services for gain.

This commercial activity may encompass illegal or non-traditional services such as prostitution, marriage-brokering, organ-trading, domestic servitude or the trading of descent-based slaves. As such, slavery, in some form or another, is likely to be involved, somewhere, in the supply chain of most large businesses and to have played a part in the production or provision of a significant number of goods or services we use every day.

"Every human being, man, woman, boy and girl, is made in God's image. God is the love and freedom that is given in interpersonal relationships, and every human being is a free person destined to live for the good of others in equality and fraternity. Every person, and all people, are equal and must be accorded the same freedom and the same dignity. Any discriminatory relationship that does not respect the fundamental conviction that others are equal is a crime, and frequently an abhorrent crime.

Therefore, we declare on each and every one of our creeds that modern slavery, in terms of human trafficking, forced labour and prostitution, and organ trafficking, is a crime against humanity. Its victims are from all walks of life, but are most frequently among the poorest and most vulnerable of our brothers and sisters. On behalf of all of them, our communities of faith are called to reject, without exception, any systematic deprivation of individual freedom for the purposes of personal or commercial exploitation; in their name, we make this declaration."

Pope Francis, *Declaration on International Day for the Abolition of Slavery, 2 December 2014*

The other modern manifestation of slavery is trafficking.

## Human trafficking

The UK Human Trafficking Centre (UKHTC) says that,

In the simplest terms, human trafficking is the movement of a person from one place to another into conditions of exploitation, using deception, coercion, the abuse of power or the abuse of someone's vulnerability. It is entirely possible to have been a victim of trafficking even if your consent has been given to being moved... [for the purpose of] exploitation... which includes prostitution and other sexual exploitation, forced labour, slavery or similar practices, and the removal of organs. Although human trafficking often involves an international cross-border element, it is also possible to be a victim of human trafficking within your own country.

There is a big difference between "human trafficking" and "people-smuggling" because illegal migrants have usually consented to being moved from one place to another even if the conditions are sometimes horrendous. Those who are trafficked have not given their consent and are being moved purely so that they can be exploited by others. The UKHTC points out that for the victims of trafficking,

Any consent they do give to make the journey in the first place is likely to have been gained fraudulently, for example with the promise of a job or a better standard of living. Whilst people-smuggling always involves illegal border-crossing and entry into another country, human trafficking for exploitation can happen within someone's own country, including Britain.

22

Various agencies say that there are about four thousand women in Britain who have been trafficked for sexual exploitation. However other agencies, including the UKHTC, say that this figure is only part of the picture and that there are more people trafficked for labour exploitation than there are for sexual exploitation. The Joseph Rowntree Foundation declared in its 2005 report that "The UK has tended to address trafficking as an issue of migration control rather than one of human rights." The same organisation says that:

Migrant workers – whether illegal migrants or legal migrants working illegally – are most at risk of slavery or slavery-like working conditions... Many come expecting certain kinds of work but end up doing others: for example, women from the Baltic States were purposely trafficked for illicit activities such as shoplifting (though they had not been told this when recruited).

UK enforcement agencies estimate there may be as many as ten thousand gangmasters operating across the various industrial sectors. Most employ migrant labour in agriculture, food processing and packing, construction, catering, leisure, hotels, cleaning, textiles, and social and health care. Many operate legally. However, thousands of migrant workers working apparently legally do so under levels of exploitation which meet the international legal definition of 'forced labour', one form of slavery.

Pope Francis described human trafficking as "an open wound on the body of contemporary society, a scourge upon the body of Christ. It is a crime against humanity." (International conference on combating human trafficking, 10 April 2014)

The first real attempt to define human trafficking was in 2000 when the UN agreed the Palermo Protocol.

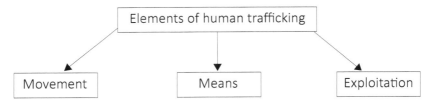

In respect of adults all three elements must be present. In respect of children (who cannot give consent) only movement and exploitation are required.

- "Movement" requires some involvement in sending, receiving or transporting people. The distance a person is moved is not important nor is whether an international border has been crossed. Trafficking within national boundaries is often referred to as domestic trafficking.
- "Means" refers to the techniques of deception, false promises, coercion, force or trickery used by traffickers to entice, encourage or force people to undertake the movement.
- "Exploitation" describes the way in which the person is abused, manipulated or used as a source of profit.

A recent report said that traffickers tell their victims not to worry if the ship meets with difficulty in the middle of the Mediterranean because they will be rescued and taken to European shores and processed. The United Nations High Commission for Refugees (UNHCR) said that, in 2017, a known 172,301 people were rescued as they tried to cross from North Africa into Europe. 3,139 died. Within the first six months of 2018, 41,381 men, women and children attempted the crossing. There were an estimated 1,063 who were declared dead or missing.

## Complexities

Many forms of slavery have more than one of the elements listed above. For example, human trafficking often involves an advance payment for travel and the promise of a job abroad, using money often borrowed from the traffickers. The existence of a debt then contributes to the control of the victims. Once they arrive at their primary destination, victims are told they cannot leave until they pay off their debt, an eventuality that, for some, may never occur. The victim experience is then one of modern slavery.

## Some facts

Due to the criminal nature of trafficking and modern slavery, combined with the definitional issues outlined above, it is impossible, with any degree of certainty, to give meaningful statistics concerning the scope, extent or scale of the problem. However, in 2017, a joint report issued by the International Labour Organization (ILO), the Walk Free Foundation and the International Organization for Migration (IOM) gave the following global figures:

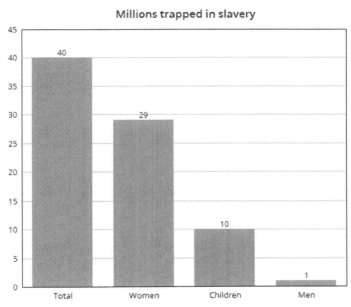

*ILO, Walk Free Foundation, 10M*

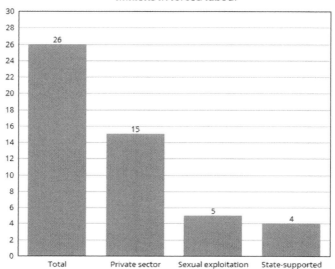

**Millions in forced labour**

*ILO, Walk Free Foundation, 10M*

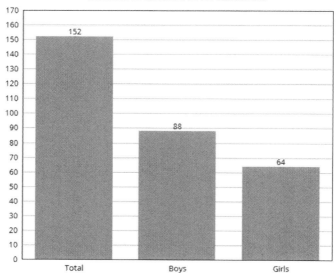

**Millions of children in forced labour**

*ILO, Walk Free Foundation, 10M*

*Forced Marriage Unit statistics 2016 – GOV.UK*

- Globally, an estimated 15.4 million people were living in a forced marriage at any moment in time in 2016. More than one third of all victims of forced marriage were children at the time of the marriage and almost all child victims were girls.

## The current situation in the UK

The UK is a destination country for men, women, and children primarily from Africa, Asia, and Eastern Europe who are subjected to human trafficking for the purposes of sexual slavery and forced labour, including domestic servitude.

Some victims, including minors from the UK, are also trafficked within the country.

Migrant workers are trafficked to the UK for forced labour in agriculture, construction, food processing, domestic servitude, and retail.

Source countries for trafficking victims in the UK include Lithuania, Poland, Albania, Slovakia, the Czech Republic, Romania, Hungary, Thailand, Vietnam, Nigeria and the People's Republic of China.

The UK is also a transit country for victims and, it has been established in the last few years, a source country, albeit on a modest scale, for victims trafficked out of the country, largely to Europe.

Accurate details about the extent of human trafficking within the UK are not available for reasons similar to those given earlier in respect of international figures. Until about 2016 the Government's position was that there were between ten and thirteen thousand victims in the UK; however, in 2017 there was a general acknowledgement that this figure was an underestimate and that the true figure may be in the tens of thousands.

Over the last few years law enforcement activity in this field has increased exponentially and at one point in 2017 there were over three hundred, separate, live investigations into the crime being mounted by police forces in the UK.

## The UK legislative picture

Until recently the legislative situation in the UK around human trafficking and modern slavery was, to say the least, a little confused. However, the Modern Slavery Act 2015 (MSA 2015) introduced recently has made things a little less opaque and it now encapsulates in law the majority of the UK's anti-slavery work.

The MSA 2015 gives law enforcement the tools to fight modern slavery, ensures perpetrators receive suitably severe punishments for their appalling crimes, and enhances support and protection for victims. It received royal assent on 26 March 2015. Whilst not without its problems the new law is a great stride forward.

The MSA 2015:

- consolidates and simplifies existing offences into a single Act
- ensures that perpetrators receive suitably severe punishments for offences including, where appropriate, life sentences

- enhances a court's ability to put restrictions on individuals where it is necessary to protect people from the harm caused by modern slavery offences
- creates an Independent Anti-slavery Commissioner (IASC) to improve and coordinate the response to modern slavery
- introduces a defence for victims of slavery and trafficking where forced criminality has taken place
- places a duty on the Secretary of State to produce guidance on victim identification and victim services
- enables the Secretary of State to make regulations relating to the identification of and support for victims
- makes provision for independent child trafficking advocates
- introduces a new reparation order to encourage the courts to compensate victims where assets are confiscated from perpetrators
- enables law enforcement to stop boats where slaves are suspected of being held or trafficked
- requires businesses over a certain size to disclose each year what action they have taken to ensure there is no modern slavery in their business or supply chains

## Human trafficking and human smuggling: similarities and differences

Human trafficking is a crime involving the exploitation of an individual for the purposes, largely, of gain.

Smuggling occurs when a person voluntarily enters into an agreement with a smuggler to gain illegal entry into a foreign country and is moved across an international border. It is defined in the Protocol against the Smuggling of Migrants by Land, Sea, and Air which supplements the UN Convention against Transnational Organized Crime.

However, not all smuggling cases involve human trafficking, nor do all cases of human trafficking begin with migrant smuggling.

# Comparing trafficking and smuggling

| Human trafficking | Migrant smuggling |
| --- | --- |
| Does not consent to being moved | Consents to being moved |
| May require fraudulent documents and transportation across national borders | May require fraudulent documents and transportation across national borders |
| Documentation usually withheld on arrival at destination | May require transportation and harbouring in destination country – factors included in the cost of transaction |
| Involves exploitation for the personal gain of the trafficker | Pays smugglers to facilitate movement, often creating large debts |
| Creates victims of crime under international law and carries entitlement to protection, services and legal redress | Does not, as such, create victims of crime under international law: migrants have paid to be moved |
| Conditions generally deteriorate on arrival and are ongoing | Transaction is generally over on arrival and full payment is made to smuggler |
| Vulnerability is increased in order to prevent escape and reporting to the authorities | Vulnerability means individuals may become victims of trafficking |
| Transported for purposes of sexual or labour exploitation | May be subjected to sex or labour trafficking in transit or on arrival at destination |
| May not be escaping violence in own country | Often escaping violence in own country |
| Prevented from contacting family or friends | May be in search of economic opportunities, better lives or to be reunited with family |
| May be passed on from one "employer" to another, usually for financial reward | Becomes vulnerable to re-exploitation |

# CHAPTER TWO

## Sexual exploitation

### Mariana's story

Mariana came to the attention of the police when a "punter" reported concerns that a prostitute he was visiting seemed unhappy, unwilling to provide services and might be trafficked. Although the police raided the brothel on three separate occasions and failed to find the girl concerned, the punter was adamant that the girl was still present.

A fourth raid was mounted. The girl was discovered hidden in a recess behind a wardrobe in one of the walls. Initially hostile and uncooperative, Mariana developed a relationship with the female investigating officer.

It emerged that Mariana was a twenty-four-year-old Roma girl from Bucharest. She was evasive about her early life and claimed to know little or nothing about her parents or any blood relations. For several years she had been living rough as part of a Roma "gang" on the streets. She claimed never to have attended school and admitted that the group had existed on the earnings from petty crime including begging, busking, pickpocketing, shoplifting and robbery.

Mariana had a "boyfriend" in Romania and it would appear that it was her boyfriend who sold her into trafficking. Initially compliant because she thought she was going to the UK to do domestic work and that her boyfriend would join her shortly, she suffered a horrific journey during which she was gang-raped and beaten.

In the UK she was forced to work for five months in a brothel before being rescued.

Initial reports from the police to the victim support service suggested that her relationships with the investigating officers were becoming unhealthy and that she was very dependent. She repeatedly stated that she was a "good girl" and had not wanted to be involved in the sex trade.

Mariana appeared slow to learn English or absorb information and was unable to resist stealing things even if they were of no value or use to her. Two initial placements at support services failed because of clashes with other victims – including a full-blown fight over Mariana's habit of "borrowing" things from others.

A medical examination revealed bruising, multiple sexually transmitted infections (STIs) and pelvic inflammatory disease (PID). Mariana refused HIV testing. She smoked heavily but there was no other evidence of substance misuse.

Mariana reacted well to authority figures but took advantage of front line staff's good nature to "test boundaries". She reacted in a sexualised and inappropriate way to men. When unsupervised she formed inappropriate relationships with men and it was a matter of some questioning as to whether Maria's behaviour was promiscuous or a re-entry into prostitution.

Trafficking and modern slavery are perhaps the most well-known form of the trade in human beings and arguably the most distressing. It is the type of exploitation that first came to the authorities' attention some years ago but, sadly, all efforts to eradicate it have so far failed.

## The sex trade in the UK

The sex trade in the UK is a diverse, thriving economy and includes prostitution, pornography, lap-dancing, striptease and explicit sexual telephone conversations to mention but part of the scenario.

This chapter will concentrate on prostitution services and to begin with it may be best to describe the trade and define some terms. It will concentrate on women selling, or being forced to sell, their services, as, to the best of our knowledge, this is the most prevalent form of the trade in the UK.

## Prostitution

"One young woman told me that she begs God for forgiveness every morning for all that she has been forced to do during the night. Then, in the evening, she also begs his pardon for all she is about to do. She came from Nigeria with the promise of work and a salary which she could send back to support her family, living in great poverty. It was only when she had passed through Passport Control at the airport and met her would-be employer that her passport, money and official papers were taken from her. For several days, she was held prisoner and given barely enough food to stay alive. Time and again, the man who collected her at the airport told her that she must repay the money it had cost to bring her from Nigeria. Until that money was paid, there would be no chance of freedom or of returning home. He threatened her, saying that if she did not agree to his proposal and tried to escape, he would notify the police that she was an illegal immigrant, so that arrest and prison would await her. She is a Catholic. For days she fought against the man's demands that she work as a prostitute. In the end, hunger drove her to accept: hunger and the need, one day, to be free to return to Nigeria."

*Sr Paula*

Prostitution in the UK may broadly be divided into "on-street" and "off-street" practices:

**On-street** – On-street prostitution services exist in most large cities of the UK, often in well-defined zones or "red-light districts" consisting of a stretch of an arterial road, a number of small side streets or around an industrial estate.

Customers for these services, often referred to as punters, access the areas by car. The women working in the environment contract for the service required and direct the punter to an area where the act can take place.

Such activity is often typified by:
- drug use by the women involved
- low charges for services
- violence from customers
- associated anti-social behaviour such as littering (particularly of condoms and drug paraphernalia) and kerb-crawling that affects other residents or users of the area

Until recently, this side of the sex trade was largely free of trafficking. However in recent years many Eastern European women have begun to appear on the streets. Some of these prostitutes are pimped. Some may be trafficked.

**Off-street** – The off-street trade can be sub-divided into a variety of sub-categories such as escort services, massage parlours, saunas, brothels and so forth, all of which are typified by the sexual acts taking place away from the public in either a fixed location or at a house or hotel of the customer's choosing.

The days of advertising these services in magazines, newsagents' windows or even with cards in telephone boxes are rapidly fading and the trade is dominated, nowadays, by the Internet.

Many of the terms used in this trade are euphemisms or are interchangeable with others but, in general terms:
- Escort services will usually arrange to meet with a client at a location of his choice or offer a house visit.

- Saunas and massage parlours operate from fixed locations under a veneer of "health services".
- Brothels are openly available in areas where there is a degree of tolerance, or less openly in areas where enforcement action is a possibility.

Again, in general terms prostitution itself is legal in the UK but almost all activities connected with it – trafficking, pimping, soliciting, kerb-crawling, living off immoral earnings, brothel-keeping and so forth are illegal.

**Specialist services** – Women often offer a variety of sexual services that pander to the varied and voracious appetites of men and may include such activities as:

- unprotected sex (without a contraceptive sheath)
- group sex with more than one prostitute
- BDSM (Bondage, Domination and Sado-Masochism)
- TV (Transvestism)
- infantilism (dressing and treating the client as a baby or child)

In addition darker, more sinister and well-hidden services exist, offering children or animals for sexual purposes.

## Non-prostitution-related sexual services

A variety of different sexual services, other than prostitution, also exists in the UK and includes:

- lap dancing
- pornography
- strip tease
- sex shows/voyeurism
- telephone chat rooms

These activities are, like prostitution, bedevilled by trafficking and coercion and form part of the wider sex trade, feeding off the inequality of the genders and the objectification of women.

## Recent case studies

Of course all of the above areas of sex work are there to be exploited by traffickers or modern day slave-owners.

### Adriana's story

"I have only been in the UK a few months and when you read this I will have returned home to my family in Romania.

My trip was arranged very quickly, a couple of months before Christmas. I got to know these two guys who offered me a good job in the UK as a cleaner. I thought it would be an opportunity to improve my English. Within two weeks my flight was booked, so I packed my bags and travelled with one of the guys, Marius, and another girl to whom he had offered a similar job.

I was really excited, although I was sad to be leaving my boyfriend and family behind. We flew into Heathrow and then a couple came to pick us up in their car to drive to a house not far from the airport.

I gave Marius my passport and my birth certificate so that he could arrange the cleaning work with an agency. The next morning when I woke up there were three men – complete strangers – at the house.

Marius told me that I was now working as a prostitute and these men were my first customers. I tried to get out of the front door but it was locked. Marius hit me across the face and told me I would have to work for him before he would let me go home.

37

The men took it in turns to rape me and after this I was locked in the bedroom. I know that they paid Marius for what they did to me, but I never saw any of the money myself.

Life continued like this, with me seeing anything from five to twelve men every day and night.

After two weeks he started to take me to brothels around central London where I would be locked into a room and forced to have sex with men over and over again. The physical pain was not the hardest thing to handle: it was the emotional hurt that left me feeling numb. This numbness eventually became my coping mechanism. I lost my fight. I gave in.

After a while, they started to trust me more and one day I said I had to get some cigarettes. I went straight to the police and told them everything. It was only after this I got the help I needed. I was taken to a safe house at the Medaille Trust. The Trust has helped me see a doctor, contact my family and arrange my safe journey home."

## Male prostitution

There is a considerable number of male prostitutes operating in the UK. Very few of these offer services to women: the trade is normally for the purposes of same-sex activities.

The number of these male prostitutes who have been trafficked or are held in conditions of modern slavery is much more difficult to assess. This is partly because, to date, there has been less serious police investigation into male, rather than female prostitution.

Significant numbers of foreign nationals, particularly from South and Latin America, are involved in male prostitution.

When examining questions around prostitution and the trafficking and slavery that are inevitably intertwined with it, it is necessary to also consider questions of "agency". It is a difficult area to explore, with passionate and emotive views held on all sides of the debate.

## What is an individual's agency?

The term "agency", in this context, describes the degree of freely given consent, or the degree of choice exercised by the person engaged in prostitution.

Many women are forced into prostitution by traffickers, pimps or unscrupulous partners. It is, however, also clear that some women engage in the trade voluntarily. Of course for a significant proportion of those who choose prostitution it is because there is no other viable choice.

Prostitution may be a coping or survival mechanism in times of poverty or hardship or indeed expected, in a particular culture or society, to be the route to be chosen by a particular class or social structure among women.

## Free to choose?

To what extent is a woman free to choose her sexual activity if
▫ sexual violence is considered "normal"?
▫ women are not considered men's equals?
▫ social pressures and expectations dictate her behaviour?

One suggested response to this state of affairs is known as the Nordic Model and is briefly discussed below.

## The Nordic Model

In its simplest form the Nordic Model might be described as:
- offering a legal solution to combat the exploitation of women
- decriminalising all those who are prostituted
- criminalising the buying of people for sex
- providing support services to help prostitutes leave their "work"

- reducing the demand that drives sex trafficking
- attempting to change society and cultures

The theory is that no woman engaged in prostitution should be penalised or victimised for being in that situation but men should be expected to control their desires and refrain from using the services of prostitutes.

It is a model of legislation based on the simple economic theory of supply and demand. If the demand from men for the services of prostitutes can be eradicated then the supply of prostitutes by traffickers and pimps will cease.

The model has been adopted in full or in modified form in Sweden, Norway, Iceland, Northern Ireland, Canada, France and, most recently, Ireland.

Reports and research on the effectiveness of its introduction present mixed findings and, to date, none of the countries mentioned has eradicated prostitution or the related trafficking.

The value or otherwise of the Nordic Model should be seen in the context of the methods used by traffickers and slavers to recruit and control their victims. Some examples of these techniques are detailed below.

## Methods of recruitment and control

Traffickers, slavers and pimps use a variety of methods to recruit and control the women and girls they "own". Some of the methods most frequently encountered are listed below.

- The use of physical force or the threat of it is still commonly encountered in this trade and can be directed, not only at the victim, but also at her family and friends.
- One of the most frequently encountered forms of both recruitment and control is known as the "lover boy" technique. This is when the victim is befriended over a period of time and sees her trafficker as a boyfriend or lover. Elaborate tales of jointly seeking a better life in the UK are often spun in the course of creating a web of psychological dependence.

- In a significant number of cases debt bondage is used as a means of maintaining control over an individual. A debt is created by facilitating migration to the UK. That debt must be paid off by working in a brothel. In many cases it can be added to over time with charges for such things as food, accommodation or interest. In some cases the debt escalates to levels at which it can never be paid off in any meaningful length of time.
- Interwoven into the techniques above, traffickers will use a certain amount of "tradecraft" to increase the dependence and reliance of the victims on them. They may be kept isolated from others, or forbidden to go out, socialise or learn English. They may have their passports and ID documents taken from them and be fed false stories about the authorities and their immigration status.
- In extreme cases there have been instances of victims being made dependent on drink or drugs as a means of control and compliance.

## The sexual exploitation of minors

It is inevitable that the trade in sexual exploitation should include children. Certainly minors (both boys and girls) are being brought to the UK for abuse but, as far as we can tell, most of this activity is domestic, with traffickers and slavers recruiting and exploiting UK citizens.

## The grooming of UK minors

A variety of recent cases across the UK has highlighted the issue of the grooming and exploitation of minors for sexual exploitation.

Undoubtedly this has been going on for many years but the recent uncovering of what amount to paedophile rings in such places as Bradford, Rochdale, Oxford, Newcastle, Manchester and Rotherham has revealed disturbing evidence of the extent of the problem.

Organised groups of men systematically target vulnerable children, many of whom are in care, and groom them with meals, drinks, drugs and attention before moving on to abuse them. Such treatment of young girls is legally classified as trafficking and the status of the children amounts to modern slavery.

## The Internet

In recent years, perhaps not unexpectedly, traffickers and slavers have made increasing use of the Internet as a tool to recruit and control their victims Before closing it may be relevant to expand on this a little.

During the past few years, much of the advertising and a great deal of the administration, such as making an appointment or paying for a service, is now done online. This offers considerable advantages to the trafficker or pimp:

- The use of technology can create safety for traffickers by placing a barrier between them and the exploited person that may be difficult for law enforcement agencies to penetrate.
- Extreme criminal activity that might attract swift and robust law enforcement activity can be concealed on the dark web behind layers of encryption.
- The use of the Internet allows criminal suppliers to reach a wide market place and offer a great deal of "consumer choice".

The continued use of technology is a growing trend which presents a whole range of new challenges to the policing of the activities described.

## Amy's story

While living in Lithuania, Amy never remembers feeling the love of a mother or father. Raised by an aunt who treated her differently from her own children, she was often beaten and made to complete gruelling chores. This caused her to suffer deep depression from a tender age and as a result she still self-harms whenever she feels unable to cope with the struggles and toils of life.

When Amy became an adult, a "friend" encouraged her to travel to the UK to work in a fruit factory and earn more money than she could in Lithuania.

In the UK the friend introduced her to other Lithuanians who seemed friendly to begin with but Amy later realised they were not as benevolent as she had first thought.

One of the ladies who had befriended her sold her. Amy was forced to marry this man she did not know and was made to live with him in a house shared by many other strangers. She was told she would be killed if she complained and there was no way of returning home.

Amy found herself alone, without any help. She had never had any relationship with a man before, so this was a terrifying experience for her. Many times her "husband" raped her. As a result of this she started to self-harm and to drink heavily to try and forget her situation.

One day her husband was out and she got drunk in the company of another man with whom she had become friendly. There was no one else in the house and the man became aggressive with her when she refused to have sex with him. He raped her and she became pregnant. Amy decided to confide in a female friend about her horrific situation and the friend encouraged her to run away.

One day Amy waited until she was alone in the house and ran away. She did not know the area and spoke only a little English so she was very nervous and fearful. Her husband had told her that if she went out without telling him, he would kill her. She knew that he saw her as his "property" because he had purchased her.

After entering a police station and asking for help, Amy was assessed and placed in the care of the Medaille Trust. She and two other survivors of modern slavery went on to be key witnesses in the prosecution against her traffickers. They bravely took the stand and testified against those responsible. Collectively the offenders were sentenced to twenty-one years in prison.

It may be relevant to note that although this chapter has concentrated on prostitution as a form of sexual exploitation it is not the only sphere of trafficking where this occurs. Rape and abuse is a common danger found in all forms of trafficking. Sexual exploitation is sexual exploitation whatever the context.

# CHAPTER THREE

## Labour exploitation

### Billy's story

Billy is from a small village named Bihor in Romania. Since finishing school he had been working occasionally for "cash in hand". He is very young and wanted to help support his family.

One day a friend told him about a good job in England, working in a car wash where he would earn £40 a day. Billy thought this was a good regular wage, was very interested and wanted to travel to the UK.

Billy travelled from Romania to the UK in a seven-seater minibus with other Romanian nationals. He was told he would need to pay £120 to make the trip, but, on arrival, was told that this fee had been increased to £550.

When in the UK his "boss" told Billy that he would have to work for only £20 a day until the whole debt of £550 was paid off. He was not given any days off and was expected to work a seven-day week, giving him no chance to rest or live freely.

Billy was placed in a house with many other men who also worked for "The Boss." He recalls the house being very dirty with hardly any furniture. He shared a bedroom with five others, sleeping on mattresses on the floor with no bed sheets. He was ordered to pay £100 per week in rent, leaving him just £40 per week for food and other expenses.

As soon as Billy arrived into the UK he had his ID card taken from him. He said he was very scared of "The Boss", saying, "He was a very big man with no hair. He was always shouting at the others and I did not want to make him angry".

Billy had been in the UK for about two months when the police raided the car wash where he was working. He was taken away by the police with six others as victims of modern slavery. The police interviewed him at the police station for about three hours. Billy gave full details of where he was living and the conditions, his earnings and how he was recruited.

He was entered into the National Referral Mechanism and taken to the Medaille Trust. Billy settled into the safe house really well and told staff that he is comfortable, feels safe and is eating well. He happily engages with other members of the household and is often seen in the company of others watching TV or going out shopping.

When he first moved into the safe house, Billy expressed an interest in staying in the UK to find legal employment but more recently he has said he would like to return to Romania.

## Introduction

As we saw in the last chapter, trafficking and modern slavery for sexual exploitation was perhaps the first crime associated with trafficking and modern slavery to come to the attention of people in the UK. Following swiftly on from that was a growing understanding that people were being transported and exploited to use the labour they could offer.

Our first understanding of this was with the use of slave labour on British farms and in the agricultural and food processing sector in general. Since then our knowledge of labour exploitation in the UK has advanced considerably. Some of what we now know is outlined below.

## Background

The term exploitation may often conjure visions of gangs working in fields or of crowded sweatshops with both involving hard manual labour, long work hours and overbearing supervisors ruling by fear.

This type of exploitation is certainly still seen in the UK and significant numbers of victims, mainly from Eastern Europe, lead a miserable existence toiling away in farms, factories and warehouses.

The exploiter's aim is to gain financially through the free or cheap labour of another person and such situations equate to a form of modern day slavery. The slave is forced to work for the enslaver often by threat, force or coercion.

In some cases the coercion can stem from an emotional attachment or perceived relationship.

Currently the largest proportion of victims exploited for labour in the UK is males, both adults and children, although women are also encountered. The number of victims discovered being used in this way continues to rise year-on-year in a shocking way despite our best efforts to prevent the crime.

The stereotypes of labour exploitation, while still valid, are by no means the total picture.

As a starting point it may be worth considering the full extent of where we are seeing exploitation and abuse of labour in the UK. The following section gives some indication of the scope of the problem.

## The areas of exploitation

Trafficking or modern slavery has been noted in the following sectors or areas of industry:

- Agriculture on our farms and small holdings
- Food processing, particularly in meat processing
- Fishing, particularly in the deep sea fleets operating out of Scotland and Northern Ireland
- Shell fishing, which continues to be an issue around the coasts of the UK
- The mercantile marine, particularly in ships using flags of convenience
- Catering in a range of establishments, including large fast food chains, Indian and Chinese restaurants and individual hotels and cafes
- The retail sector with its large workforce has been the centre of several police investigations into both small and large firms.
- Construction firms and sites offer great opportunities with the nature of how they work - the temporary, transitory, sub-contracting methods used are fertile ground for exploiters.
- Car washes: these areas of exploitation are talked of in a little more detail later.
- Nail bars and the beauty industry are areas of concern around trafficking and modern slavery and briefly examined below.
- The care sector is providing increasing evidence of widespread abuses of the large, low-paid workforce with its significant proportion of foreign workers.
- The scrap metal and recycling trades have always been tainted with a degree of criminality. Traffickers and slavers have been quick to spot the opportunities presented.

- Cleaning (domestic and industrial) is again a sector employing significant numbers of foreign nationals on low wages with limited rights and is a breeding ground for exploitation.
- Home working on the textile or packaging trade is an area of work that is open to abuse and considerable concerns have been expressed about certain working practices in the East Midlands that appear to abuse certain, largely Asian, parts of some communities.

This list is by no means exhaustive or comprehensive. In order to illustrate this better we shall take a brief look in a little more detail at four areas.

**Car washes** – the recent burgeoning of low-priced, hand car washes in the UK has been a phenomenon in recent years. Services are often delivered cheaply from run-down, low-rent sites.

**Nail bars** – a similar story lies behind many of the rash of nail bars that have appeared on high streets across the UK in recent years. Staffed in many cases by young Vietnamese workers, they offer low-cost services to a hungry market of female service consumers who often do not question the origin or background of the staff. It is an industry acknowledged to be heavily tainted by the use of slave labour or trafficking victims who are often controlled by high levels of debt bondage.

**Farms** – despite increased regulation and the work of the Gang-masters and Labour Abuse Authority (GLAA) the abuse of, largely, foreign workers from the EU on UK farms seems to be a continuing problem. As well as exploiting cheap labour, the farms involved in these practices are often guilty of a variety of other offences such as incorrectly labelling or re-labelling produce, ignoring health and safety rules or tax avoidance.

**Ships** – it is only within the last few years that we have noticed the significant levels of abuse in the fishing industry operating out of UK ports and the wider mercantile marine, both operating from and transiting UK waters. Overseas mariners, often from the Philippines, West Africa or Eastern Europe are held on ships, often in appalling conditions for little or no pay, for periods of months or, in some cases, years. Clauses included in the Modern Slavery Act of 2015 were designed to increase the investigative abilities of the authorities in connection with these matters but it is safe to say that, at present, we have not uncovered the full extent of the problem, let alone countered it.

Before moving on from this brief summary of labour exploitation it may be of interest to discuss the use, by certain traveller groups, of exploited labour. This has featured heavily in the press over recent years as the case study shown below illustrates:

### Albert's story

"I have never married nor had children. I enjoyed working hard in a cleaning business and I have always lived with my mother. When I turned fifty-seven my mother died and everything went wrong for me. I was unable to cope emotionally and eventually became unemployed and that soon led to homelessness.

Two men approached me near a night shelter and offered me work, food, accommodation and alcohol. I said 'yes'. I was made to share a damp caravan with three others and had to do landscaping work from 6am to 10pm six days per week.

I never received any money for the work I did.

I was really frightened of the men. They beat me up. They moved me on to another traveller site when they were bored with me... For four more years I continued to live like this!

Eventually, the police helped me when they raided the caravan site. A very nice policewoman made me feel safe and eventually I felt safe enough to begin explaining what had happened to me.

The police told me of a charity that helps people like me and offered me a place in a safe house. The Medaille Trust looked after me for several months and helped me get back on my feet. I now know more of what happened to me and realise that the group who had me, sold me on several times. They were also claiming benefits for me illegally and pocketing the cash themselves.

Finally, there is hope and I'm rebuilding my life. The thing that might surprise you about me is my nationality: I am British."

The appalling story of many years of slavery may be shocking and it is difficult to accept that such things happen in the UK. It may also be appropriate to warn against vilifying a particular community or group of people such as travellers. As the next case study shows, a cultural group can be victims as much as anyone else:

## The Travellers' story

Suzie and John, a married couple in their early forties, are from a large English travelling community in rural England. They were recently rescued in a police raid that freed them from fourteen years of captivity, forced unpaid labour and horrendous abuse at the hands of a violent and controlling travelling family.

It all began in 1999, when the well-known family bought a plot of land next to the one where Suzie, John and Bob had been comfortably living for a few years. They had many ambitious plans for the area and pulled their trailers and animals onto the site to begin life there.

The matriarch of the family, Dixie, was a cousin of Suzie's. She began inviting Suzie and the boys over to her trailer to socialise. John and Bob were offered all sorts of labouring jobs, helping the family to set up their land and tend to their animals. Suzie was offered cleaning jobs and helped Dixie with her shopping and general chores. They were all paid fairly and, for a while, life seemed to be going well. After six months of paid work, Suzie and John were asked if they wanted to pull their trailer onto the land, so they did. Not long after, Bob's marriage broke down and he also moved onto the land.

Suzie, John and Bob lived on the land, worked for the family and any other time was spent going round to traveller shows and helping Dixie and family with jobs and errands.

The good times were short-lived. It soon became apparent that their lives were not their own. Not only were they not free to do anything they wanted, but the pay rapidly dropped off. There were always reasons for why they weren't being paid. Tax, insurance, repairs and new tyres were all typical excuses.

The work became harder, more unpleasant and more unfair. John owned a pony and several animals of his own. They were neglected as he was too busy looking after the family's animals. The day would start at 6.30am, cleaning up the mess of the family's fighting dogs. Also on site were chickens, ducks, turkeys, horses, fighting birds and a cannabis plantation.

The three people would find themselves with no money and living off scraps, leftovers and out-of-date food, thrown at them by Dixie's family. They suffered violence, humiliation and a lack of freedom at the hands of this evil family.

Other incidents included Bob being forced to cut off a fighting dog's ears and, when he refused, having his hand lacerated. He gave in and begrudgingly performed the mutilation.

Also, Dixie would take any groceries obtained from the food bank. She would select the best products for herself and take benefits straight from their accounts.

It all became too much for Bob who dared to run away in 2006. He decided to return when news reached him that Suzie and John's trailer had been burnt down in retaliation for his absconding.

Suzie and John were forced to live in a small touring trailer for two years and when an adequate trailer was bought for them, there was absolutely no pay as anything they earned went straight to paying off the trailer. The debt never went down.

In 2010, John felt he had been pushed to a point where he could take no more and set fire to himself. He was hosed down and refused medical treatment for his terrible burns. A year later he attempted to hang himself from a tree but was rescued by Bob who found him.

The enslaving family had been involved in other criminal activity which had alerted police, who had been gathering evidence for some time before the raid early on a February morning of 2014.

The police banged on the door and confirmed the identity of the three victims. Dixie, her husband, two sons and a daughter were all handcuffed and taken away. The police found a place for the three victims to rest and recuperate after their ordeal.

They were transported to a Medaille Trust safe house in another part of the country where they were at last able to recover. Following good nutrition, medical help and emotional support from Medaille staff, they have finally been allowed to be themselves and, most importantly, regain their freedom. Bob said he feels like he has been given his life back and is looking forward to moving into a two-bedroomed property alongside Suzie and John.

## Children and families

Another aspect of the trafficking of people for forced labour is the use of children in certain industries around the UK. These are often between twelve and seventeen years of age and their use as child labourers is often only part of the abusive experience they suffer, with sexual abuse also commonly occurring. Child victims have been recovered from farms, shops, nail bars and car washes.

Another situation we are seeing more commonly is the exploitation of whole families.

A family is trafficked into the UK, often from Eastern Europe, with traffickers seeking to maximise their potential income. Once in the UK and under the control of their traffickers, adult males may be put to work in factories, young girls forced into prostitution, very young children used for begging purposes and older children groomed for future roles in the sex trade. The identities of the whole family may also be stolen for the purposes of fraudulent benefit claims. This type of mixed exploitation may involve large familial grouping of several generations.

## The Gangmasters and Labour Abuse Authority (GLAA)

Before closing this chapter, mention should be made of the GLAA. This Government body was set up following the Morecambe Bay disaster of 2004 during which the lives of at least twenty-one trafficking victims from China were lost.

The Authority's initial remit was to look at the licensing of gangmasters in the agriculture, shellfish and food processing industries. Recently its remit has been widened and it is now a key agency involved in the fight against modern slavery. Arguably still under-resourced, it continues to investigate crimes across the UK, police and regulate in key areas of concern, and attempt to make the UK a hostile environment for traffickers.

# CHAPTER FOUR

## Domestic servitude

"Alongside this deeper cause – the rejection of another person's humanity – there are other causes which help to explain contemporary forms of slavery. Among these, I think in the first place of poverty, underdevelopment and exclusion, especially when combined with a lack of access to education or scarce, even non-existent, employment opportunities. Not infrequently, the victims of human trafficking and slavery are people who look for a way out of a situation of extreme poverty; taken in by false promises of employment, they often end up in the hands of criminal networks which organize human trafficking. These networks are skilled in using modern means of communication as a way of luring young men and women in various parts of the world."

*Pope Francis, Message for the World Day of Peace, 1 January 2015*

## Yvette's story

Yvette came to the UK on a holiday visa. A family friend arranged her visa and told her that they would meet her at the airport. They also paid for her ticket. The traffickers collected her at the airport and took her to their house, where many people were living, about five to each room.

The family then made her work from 6am until 2am in the morning without any breaks. They forced her to cook and wash for them and did not pay her for the work. She had to clean the house and another house they had, carry out garden chores, do their washing and ironing and clean their cars. They verbally and physically abused Yvette, who has many scars from her experience. She was beaten with sticks and belts and burnt with cigarettes. The traffickers told her nothing about this country and locked the doors, forbidding her to go out. Yvette was deprived of food and sometimes water. She became very weak and malnourished.

Following two years of captivity, Yvette managed to escape through a window that had been left open. In a nearby park, she met a man who said he would help her as he said he knew how she was living. However, instead of helping Yvette, he sexually abused her and then threw her out onto the street.

When she arrived at the safe house, Yvette was very thin and malnourished, dirty, unkempt and very tired. At first, we had to ensure she followed a careful, limited diet until she could tolerate food properly. We bought her clothes, shoes and personal items, as she arrived – like most – with nothing. We encouraged her to sleep, eat and recuperate.

When Yvette was well enough, the Medaille Trust slowly got her used to going outside again among other people as she was very scared and felt unsafe. She was very mentally confused and, at times, could not talk coherently or sensibly with staff and would laugh manically. She has accessed the sexual health clinic and seen a GP and dietician.

Yvette has also recently started volunteering in a local charity shop, a job which she is really enjoying. She has started to smile and, although her future is difficult, she wishes to try to stay in the UK, rebuild her life and, one day, feel safe and happy again.

## What is domestic servitude?

Domestic servitude is the seemingly normal practice of household help that is used as cover for the exploitation and control of someone, usually from another country.

It is a form of forced labour, but it also warrants its own category of slavery because of the unique contexts and challenges it presents.

Domestic workers in domestic servitude work inside private households, do not have any legal protection and will perform a range of tasks in private homes including, but not limited to, cooking, cleaning, laundry, taking care of children and the elderly and running errands. Some domestic workers also live in their employers' homes and are often considered "on call" to undertake work for their employer twenty-four hours a day. The pay is often very low, with wage payments frequently delayed. Some domestic workers may not be paid at all or only receive "payment in kind" such as food or accommodation.

For some domestic workers, the circumstances and conditions of their work will fall within the definition of slavery already discussed in this book. This happens when employers stop domestic workers from leaving the house, do not pay wages, use violence or threats, withhold their identity documents, limit their contact with family and force them to work.

A case in the last twenty years which is perhaps most in the public conscience is that of Victoria Climbié who found herself in a situation of domestic servitude during the catalogue of abuse that occurred during her short life.

There are many high profile cases in recent years of domestic servitude, and its preponderance as a form of exploitation is over-represented in the households of some cultures. We will discuss this in more detail later in this chapter.

## Janet's story

"My parents died when I was very young so a woman brought me up in Uganda. I had no siblings. I went to school for a short while but soon had to work full-time in the fields for a farmer because we could not afford for me to attend school.

One day when I was thirteen and working in the fields, three teenage boys raped me, resulting in a pregnancy. Unfortunately, the baby died inside me at five months but it was not until three days later when they were able to remove it. Much of my uterus was removed also as there was a problem with it. I have had irregular and heavy periods since then and I believe I cannot conceive again.

I came to the UK through a woman who befriended my "mother" and encouraged her to let me go to the UK to be a nanny for her. She said she had lived in the UK for years and had three young children who needed care. She made all of the ID and travel arrangements and I arrived here in early 2007, not being able to speak a word of English.

She would invite male friends around for dinner and they would eat and get drunk together. Because there was no lock on my door they would regularly come in at night and force me to sleep with them. I shouted and screamed but the woman never came to help me. I would ask her the next day why she let this happen and she would slap me and tell me that I had to pay for the roof over my head.

I managed to get away after about two years. The woman who had kept me in her house announced that she and the family were going to America. She put me out on the street, locked the house up and drove away. I knew no one and my English was very limited as the words I had picked up were from interacting with the children. I walked and sat on buses to keep warm. I had no idea what to do and was terrified that I would be arrested. I was taken in eventually by a kind man whom I met on a bus. He looked after me until recently."

The stories of Yvette and Janet show that domestic slavery can last for many years, the "employer" successfully hiding the deceit from third parties. Whilst Yvette and Janet are now trying to form better lives, their former hardship is not "over and done with". They need the help and support of various NGOs if they are to cope with the long-lasting effects of their slavery and be successfully and happily rehabilitated.

## Culturally acceptable or just abuse?

Both Yvette and Janet came from African countries and were brought into the UK. It is not uncommon for a number of individuals in domestic servitude to come from Africa or South Asia into the UK – but what are the reasons behind this?

## Context in the UK

To put the issue into context, the trafficking of persons from various African countries and outside of Africa to Europe – including the UK – is a growing problem.

Experts in Africa have suggested that at least one million African children are victims of trafficking and exploitation (all forms of trafficking and not only for domestic servitude) within Africa itself. Similar statistics regarding domestic servitude are found in the Indian subcontinent.

The International Labour Organisation (ILO) estimated the number of domestic maids employed in India surged by nearly seventy per cent between 2001 and 2010, many with limited rights and conditions of work.

Domestic assistants and servants are not a new phenomenon and have been commonplace in all cultures and times, including the UK, and especially during the time of the British Empire. Colonial heritage is a key reason for the above ethnicities being seen more frequently in the UK but there are also other factors which may stem from certain cultural hangovers or beliefs:

61

- poverty and the need for employment
- cultural acceptance of domestic service and treatment of such workers
- gender inequality: acceptance that daughters will be sent away more readily (see section on Restavek below) – human trafficking most often affects women and children in impoverished areas
- lack of legal framework, minimum payment and worker rights
- lack of unions or voice and an awareness of the occurrence of domestic servitude
- a belief that joining a family that is known to the victim might be an opportunity to
  - earn and provide for others
  - receive an education if a child
  - have a better life than the one being left behind

> BUT IT CAN OCCUR ANYWHERE,
> WHETHER LABELLED AS CULTURE OR ABUSE

Forced domestic servitude also occurs in the United States. There have been several cases of various legal and undocumented workers traveling to the US under the pretence of real employment and then forced into enslavement.

One such example is the story of Maria and Sandra Bearden of Laredo, Texas. In *The Slave Next Door*, we learn of Sandra, an upper-middle-class mother with a solid brick home and manicured lawn. She wanted a housemaid and nanny but did not want to pay a lot for the services. She travelled to Mexico where she promised a set of parents that she would provide an education for their daughter in the United States. She smuggled their daughter, Maria, into the US and immediately imprisoned her in Texas.

Sandra, currently serving a life sentence for trafficking in persons, sprayed Maria with pepper spray, hit her with brooms and bottles and sexually assaulted her with a gardening tool. Sandra even chained Maria to a pole in the backyard and fed her dog faeces. An attentive neighbour finally saw Maria in the backyard and reported the crime to authorities.

## Restavek

"Restavek" is a type of human trafficking. It takes children from their home, promises them something in exchange for a move away from home and exploits them in their most vulnerable state.

There are 250,000 children in Restavek. Two-thirds are girls.

There are many reasons as to why domestic servitude can continue and flourish. In certain communities, there is a belief that it may be an escape from poverty, an opportunity to earn money and to provide for families elsewhere.

"Employers" may abuse the system simply because they can. Where there is no legal framework, no opportunity for a victim to disclose the circumstances of his/her situation and a tacit acceptance by communities, then domestic bondage will continue.

Haiti is an example of how domestic servitude is permitted to continue, almost on an acceptable basis. Whilst it has arisen from a complex historical situation and from the fact the sixty-one per cent of Haitians live below the poverty line, it does not make it right.

In the Creole language, "restavek" means "to stay with". In Haiti, it describes the situation in which children from rural areas are sent to families in the urban districts. In theory, restavek allows urban families to gain help with their daily lives and provides rural children with an opportunity for education. For rural families, it is one less child to feed where they are unable to provide for the child's basic needs.

In reality, the children are treated as little more than slaves and do not have access to education or fair treatment.

## Diplomatic immunity

Supermodel Waris Dirie, in her book *Desert Flower*, talks briefly about her life as a servant in a diplomatic household. Whilst this book was written in 1998, there are still many cases of diplomatic households exploiting individuals in 2018 and hiding behind diplomatic immunity.

Although employers are seeking Domestic Workers in a Private Household Visas, those in diplomatic service are not always accorded the employee rights that such visas should allow.

Each year, between sixteen and seventeen thousand "potentially vulnerable" domestic workers are given entry clearance to the UK. From 2003 to 2011, approximately seventy-six per cent of these workers were women. Overseas domestic workers are typically required to carry out a range of tasks including cleaning, cooking, providing childcare and laundry services. Male domestic workers are often brought to the UK as drivers, cooks and private security guards. These workers predominantly originate from Africa and Asia, especially the Philippines, India and Indonesia. But the majority of workers enter the UK from a country that is not their country of origin, in particular from Saudi Arabia, Bahrain, Oman, Qatar, and the UAE.

Many of these workers work under a "kafala" arrangement, which is widespread in the Gulf region. "Kafala" legally ties migrant workers to their employers so the workers are not permitted to leave their jobs or the country without their employer's permission.

In October 2017, two domestic workers who say they were exploited by a diplomat in London, won a major victory in the Supreme Court after judges ruled that their employer was no longer protected by diplomatic immunity.

The two women worked at a diplomatic residence in London. They were expected to work for eighteen hours a day, seven days a week and were not allowed to leave the house unless escorted by family members.

The Supreme Court ruled that employing a domestic worker could not be said to fall within a diplomat's official functions, so any diplomatic immunity was lost when they ceased to be in post.

Diplomats bring an estimated two to three hundred migrant domestic workers into the UK each year.

The Supreme Court decision came after a challenge brought by the charity the Anti-Trafficking and Labour Exploitation Unit (ATLEU). It also implies that, in similar cases, immunity would not apply to diplomats even while they were in post. A majority of the Court accepted the argument that, because trafficking was a commercial activity, outside of a diplomat's official role, the usual diplomatic protections would not apply under any circumstances.

"These appeals are hugely significant. Overseas domestic workers working in diplomatic households and embassies are exceptionally vulnerable to exploitation and abuse, including trafficking. We would urge the Government to take the lead in the international community and press for an amendment to the Vienna Convention on Diplomatic Relations, putting the matter of immunity in these circumstances beyond doubt.

In the meantime the Government must ensure that all domestic workers entering the UK for service with diplomats are formally employed by State Embassies rather than individual diplomats as a condition of their visas being granted. A State will enjoy no immunity in such circumstances, given the Supreme Court's separate ruling in the case of Benkharbouche v Sudan and Janah v Libya, also handed down today."

*Emmy Gibbs of ATLEU, 18 October 2017*

## How is control maintained?

There are numerous methods of control that traffickers can exert over their victims but the most common are:

- physical control through physical beatings and violence
- emotional by way of promises of love and alleged emotional support
- psychological control whereby traffickers will use the vulnerabilities of the victim to maintain control – vulnerabilities such as harm to the families, parents and children; taking advantage of their illegal status or lack of documentation; or representations of what they may do to the victim themselves if they try to escape
- family debt bondage
- witchcraft: a belief in witchcraft and its associated rituals and curses is a daily fact of life in many developing countries and should not be underestimated. There have been many cases across Europe where victims have had to be "freed" from the witchcraft in order to be free of the mantle of being a trafficked victim

### Stockholm Syndrome

Stockholm Syndrome is a form of bonding between a captive and captor in which the captive begins to identify with, and may even sympathise with, the captor. Its name refers to the taking of four hostages during a bank robbery in Stockholm, Sweden in 1973. Following their release from captivity, the hostages defended their captors and refused to testify against them in court.

Stockholm Syndrome can occur in trafficked victims who may become dependent on the abuser, no matter what their circumstances. They believe that they cannot survive without the protection and support of their abuser and some victims might experience threats to their family and believe they are responsible for the safety of others around them.

Many complex issues may prevent a trafficked victim leaving their trafficker:

- persistent exploitation of a victim's low self-esteem
- nurture of belief that only the victim's trafficker can protect them
- victim persuaded that grooming, trafficking, giving of drugs is a needed act of kindness
- victim becomes aligned to their trafficker

## Signs of domestic slavery

Factors that may indicate that someone is a victim of domestic slavery are if they:

- live and work for a family in a private home but do not eat with them
- have no bedroom or proper sleeping place
- have no private space
- are malnourished
- never leave the house without the "employer"
- work excessive hours and are "on call" twenty-four hours a day
- are reported as missing or accused of crime by their "employer" if they try to escape

## In summary

Domestic servitude:

- happens in a wide variety of circumstances
- can require different regulatory or policy responses to prevent trafficking and provide remedies
- is shaped by a social environment, its social norms and values, discriminatory attitudes
- undervalues domestic work
- treats victims with contempt
- happens where there is a lack of policies, and gaps in protection or lack of enforcement

- is hard to monitor because labour inspectors
  - cannot conduct house visits without a warrant
  - requires substantive evidence
- requires a multi-pronged response, including criminal, labour and migration policies
- needs changes in social norms and employers' behaviour, beliefs and attitudes to address what drives exploitation
- needs exploiting employers and private households to be held accountable

**References**

Dirie W (1998) *Desert Flower*, New York, William Morrow.
Bales K and Soodalter R (2009) *The Slave Next Door*, California, University of California Press.

# CHAPTER FIVE
## Other forms of exploitation

"Another cause of slavery is *corruption* on the part of people willing to do anything for financial gain. Slave labour and human trafficking often require the complicity of intermediaries, be they law enforcement personnel, state officials, or civil and military institutions. This occurs when money, and not the human person, is at the centre of an economic system…

Further causes of slavery include *armed conflicts, violence, criminal activity* and *terrorism*. Many people are kidnapped in order to be sold, enlisted as combatants, or sexually exploited, while others are forced to emigrate, leaving everything behind: their country, home, property and even members of their family. They are driven to seek an alternative to these terrible conditions even at the risk of their personal dignity and their very lives; they risk being drawn into that vicious circle which makes them prey to misery, corruption and their baneful consequences."

*Pope Francis, Message for the World Day of Peace, 1 January 2015*

## Introduction

The previous three chapters have looked at the most common, and perhaps most familiar, forms of exploitation that victims of human trafficking or modern slavery suffer from – labour exploitation, sexual exploitation and domestic servitude.

However there are many other forms of exploitation that feature in human trafficking and modern slavery stories once we get beyond our preconceptions of what a victim should be and in what circumstances they should be found.

For ease of reference, other forms of exploitation are listed below under sub-headings that are not exhaustive. Traffickers can be cunning and innovative and there is no limit to what forms of exploitation we might see in the future.

In whatever way they can, traffickers and slavers will

- exploit the misery of others for their personal gain
- look for the lowest risk and highest return
- change their methods in response to changing operating conditions

### Working the street scene

"They practise 'rent a baby' so that one baby might have several 'mothers' in the course of a day. The baby is drugged so that it is always sleeping: after all, is there anything more beautiful than a sleeping child? Each 'mother' then spends several hours begging on the streets."

*Felicity*

"I've seen the rooms where these Bangladeshi men are kept, perhaps twelve to a small room and sleeping in bunks. They will take it in turns for two of

> them to stay behind each day to cook for the others. The others go out and sell fake designer handbags and jewellery to the tourists. Before sending money to their families, they have to pay their 'landlord' an exorbitant rent. They must also pay protection money to the Mafia who are always watching them. The Mafia warn them if the police are approaching, so they gather up their goods and run, only to return when the police have gone. There is almost no money left at the end of the day for these men to send anything to their families and so they are forced to keep on going. Sometimes the Mafia have threatened to kill their families and because the men don't know whether or not this is possible, they stay, just to keep their loved ones alive."
>
> *Fr Ben*

One of the most visible forms of exploitation to be seen, by the aware and informed observer, is the use of victims by criminals to generate income from involvement in what may be termed "street life" or low-level criminal activities.

As an example of this, begging is perhaps the most unsurprising example.

In major urban conurbations, and many smaller towns, a proportion of the individuals begging, both UK and foreign national citizens, are likely to be controlled by gangs who demand that all or a significant part of the day's "take" is handed over.

Children and babies are sometimes present in this scenario to provide "window-dressing", designed to increase the daily haul of donations from an unsuspecting public.

As the primary aim of these gangs is to generate easy income it is unsurprising that begging is not the only part of the street scene to be infiltrated: leaflet distributors, telephone box carders (advertising prostitution services), newspaper vendors, *Big Issue* sales people and windscreen car washers at road junctions and traffic lights are often also being exploited by traffickers or abusive slave masters.

Sometimes people are sent on to the streets with just a target of income required for the day to avoid a beating or earn a meal.

From begging and street trading at one end of a spectrum, this exploitation of the street environment in cities extends to some low-level crime such as shoplifting, pickpocketing, mobile phone theft and purse snatching, together with intelligence gathering for more planned, less opportunistic crimes such as burglaries.

The victims of human trafficking may be sent out to shoplift to order, to steal phones and purses from the inattentive in cafes, bars or shops. Where the individuals concerned have pickpocketing skills or these can be taught, this may well be exploited.

In terms of intelligence, victims of trafficking may be required to observe the patterns of life of vulnerable individuals, spy on ATM sites, try and collect PIN numbers or "case" premises for burglaries or robberies.

Other areas that attract this type of acquisitive crime are metal theft and the scrap trade in general.

Add to this licensed and unlicensed trading in illicit items such as pirated CDs and DVDs or counterfeit designer items such as watches, clothes or handbags in street markets and from door to door, and the trafficking gangs have created a toxic mix of petty crime.

In addition, many victims are so poorly looked after or so badly treated by their traffickers that they are forced into criminality as a means of survival or as a coping mechanism.

There have been many cases that have come to light through shoplifting of groceries, toiletries and clothes by victims so that they could simply survive the situation in which they find themselves.

As will be seen in the next chapter some victims also self-medicate with drugs or alcohol as a coping mechanism, or engage in survival sex.

Any or all of these activities may add to the general criminality or anti-social behaviour in a particular area.

## The mystery of the chewing gum thefts….

An unexplained spate of petty shoplifting from corner shops and supermarkets in a London borough seemed unconnected to human trafficking until it was investigated more deeply. It seems Romanian traffickers controlled a gang of individuals, including children, whom they put to work begging and stealing on the streets. People were given a financial target for the day: they were told that if they were coming up "short" they were to shoplift chewing gum or bubble gum to mitigate the possibility of a beating.

Chewing gum and bubble gum from leading brands is prized in Romania and often sells for a higher price than in the UK. These items, along with sweets, are often also used in lieu of change in some shops in Romania to avoid dealing in coinage. The traffickers would collect all the stolen gum and ship it back to Romania using vans going through the port at Dover.

## Forced criminality

It is just a short step from exploiting the street environment in the UK to moving into more organised, more skilled and more profitable criminal activities to exploit victims.

Perhaps the most high-profile example of forced criminality is the use of, largely Vietnamese, individuals in the cultivation and guarding of illegally grown cannabis. Throughout the UK cannabis is grown to fuel the drug trade. Whilst some of this cultivation takes place on remote farms or in industrial buildings, a proportion is grown in residential streets in towns with houses converted by having heating, lighting and irrigation systems installed to grow the plants. These systems often need monitoring and the crop needs guarding (largely from rival drug dealers) so a "gardener" is installed in the property. Experience and police investigation has shown these are often victims of trafficking.

Another example of the type of crime modern slaves and trafficking victims are forced into is the practice of bogus charity collections, a problem that first came to light in Scotland with a gang from Lithuania that was exploiting its own countrymen and -women.

The collections may be door-to-door requests for cash for a bogus charity, or indeed a bona fide cause, which, needless to say, never sees any of the proceeds.

A more familiar method is the collection of donated clothing and textiles via plastic sacks distributed and collected on certain days. The clothing never reaches a charity but is simply sold on by weight for ragging.

Traffickers may also use certain methods in the pursuit of profit from "white collar" crime around fraud and deception:
- forced labour in the catering, leisure and retail businesses
- card skimming
- theft of financial details from the public with whom they deal
- false insurance claims, often connected to claims of whiplash injuries in fake, staged or engineered motor vehicle accidents.

The aim of the traffickers in these forced criminality situations is not only to maximise income from their illicit activities but also to reduce risk to themselves by placing victims in the forefront of high-risk situations that are likely to provoke police action. All too often law enforcement fails to see the additional victims present in a particular crime investigation and victims end up being treated as perpetrators. When this happens the victim effectively acts as a "cut-off" and the investigation never gets further than the rounding up of the foot soldiers rather than the criminal gang leaders further up the hierarchy.

### Just when you think you have seen it all...

As a result of an investigation into a traveller site where slaves were being held, an illegal trade in stolen dogs was discovered. The travellers would target large mansions and country houses known to have a dog or dogs, offering, in time-honoured fashion, tarmacking and labouring services.

When asked to leave they would politely comply but not before engaging the owner in conversation about his dog. People love talking about their dogs and often answer questions about its age, training and pedigree. At a later date the travellers would task one or more of their slaves to return and steal the dog or dogs, placing all the risk of arrest on them.

Once stolen the dogs were checked for microchips which, if found, were removed (without anaesthetic). False EU Pet Passports were obtained and the stolen dogs were transported to the continent for sale in Germany where trained working dogs such as springer spaniels, labradors and retrievers command high prices, often on a no-questions-asked basis.

Another disturbing trend being seen in the use of victims by criminal gangs is their increasing use in aspects of the drug trade beyond the cannabis cultivation scenario. There is growing evidence that victims of trafficking are being used as "mules" to bring drugs into the UK. There is also forced involvement in the street trade as couriers, lookouts and sellers of a variety of hard drugs being distributed by organised crime gangs of both foreign and domestic origin.

## Sham marriages

The term "sham marriages" is an umbrella term which covers a variety of marriage abuses engineered by traffickers and slavers; other terms include bogus, forced, fixed, arranged and involuntary depending upon the circumstances.

Where the sole purpose of the marriage is to obtain a slave this aspect is discussed later in this chapter.

Most frequently seen in the UK is the marriage of someone who is not an EU citizen or whose ethnic origin is non-EU to an EU national. Most commonly, this is to obtain some advantage for the purchaser of the marriage in terms of their immigration status, or that of their dependants in one or more of the EU states.

Typically, the woman involved in the sham marriage will have been trafficked for the purpose. She may, over the course of time, contract many such false arrangements.

However, some examples have been seen of women, seeking to gain advantage, marrying exploited men.

## Identity theft, benefit fraud and money laundering

Perhaps the most common form of trafficking exploitation seen in the UK is also, perhaps, the most under-reported.

Traffickers are interested in making money and the murky world of criminal finance and fraud provides a fertile operating environment.

In respect of EU citizens, one of the easiest and most lucrative forms of exploitation is to make victims complete and submit false claims for benefits and tax credits. It represents a very low-risk but high-return activity for criminals and takes advantage of the UK bureaucracies for such claims which are widely acknowledged to be weak and vulnerable to organised attack.

The scale of false claims, particularly within the child benefit and tax credit systems, is truly staggering, with one police force estimating the loss to the UK from such organised crime attacks to be in excess of one billion pounds. Within that sum a proportion of the theft and fraud will have been perpetrated by traffickers using either their victims' stolen personal details or the coerced victim acting directly as a front for a false claim.

The problem of identity theft is widespread amongst trafficked populations. Stolen identities are used, not only for false benefit claims, but also to obtain false documents, loans and credit cards, perpetrate the type of insurance frauds and sham marriages outlined earlier, and facilitate travel and "clean" footprints for criminals and money launderers.

The laundering of money through UK businesses and banks takes place on a huge scale and traffickers play a significant part in this. It is extremely rare to meet an EU victim of trafficking who has not, at some stage in their trafficking experience, opened or been forced to open a bank account, the details and control of which have passed to a criminal enterprise.

This area of "white collar" exploitation of victims remains under-reported and under-investigated yet, probably, accounts for the majority of trafficking in the UK.

## Organ removal and egg harvesting

To date, the horrific trade in humans for organ removal and sale has, thankfully, not figured highly in the activities of criminal gangs operating in the UK. However there are some disturbing indications that it may be on the current and future agenda of some individuals or groups.

Victims in debt bondage situations have related that traffickers have suggested "giving" a kidney as a means of paying off their debt and obtaining their freedom.

The UK immigration services have also stopped and spoken to several individuals leaving the UK to travel to the Middle East or the Indian sub-continent where they have suspected that the purpose of the journey is to sell, voluntarily or otherwise, an organ.

Another form of trafficking and exploitation that we could expect to see at some stage is the illegal harvesting of human eggs from victims for sale for research or fertilisation purposes. Elsewhere in Europe this has been reported, with investigations on trade taking place between Bulgaria and Greece. It seems probable that this trade in human organs will, at some stage, appear in the UK.

### Witchcraft rituals

"The woman had completely 'lost it'. A few days previously and without her knowledge, her husband sold their five-year-old daughter to a 'businessman' for her heart for the equivalent of about £4. What made it worse was that the child's heart had to be cut out whilst she was still alive. The mother just had a complete mental breakdown when she found out."

*Maria*

There is a worldwide trade in objects for use in the witchcraft rituals associated with certain animist and other religions.

These may be simple fetish objects of a mineral or vegetable origin but a significant trade in animal parts has also been noted.

In extreme cases this can involve the trafficking of human beings for use in rituals that can involve murder.

## "Just slavery"

Some individuals seek to own a slave for the primary purpose, not of exploitation, but simply for the exercise of power and their particular perversions.

There have been several recorded instances where individuals, normally men, have sought to purchase an individual from a criminal gang or a middleman, as a slave, simply for the gratification of owning one.

A sham marriage may be involved; sexual exploitation is a given and unremitting domestic labour for the benefit of the owner is expected. Slave owners may also seek to gain an income from their slave by putting them into paid employment in the legal market or in the "black" economy.

Whatever other benefits may accrue, the defining common denominator is the desire of one individual to exercise power and total control over another. Multiple exploitation of a victim, which is discussed below, inevitably follows once control of an individual has been established.

## Multiple exploitation

One of the aims of this book is to raise the level of awareness concerning human trafficking and modern slavery, but this can only truly be achieved if readers gain some insight into the complex, nuanced and often episodic nature of the phenomena. Many cases that come to the attention of NGOs or the authorities do not fall neatly into a category of, say, sexual or labour exploitation or even one of the categories outlined in this chapter.

### What sort of exploitation is this?

Precious was brought to the UK from Tanzania to be a domestic servant for a family. During the evening she cooks, cleans and cares for the family. During the day, after she drops the children at school, she is made to work in a sweet shop. Almost every night, after the wife retires, she is raped by the woman's husband.

Traffickers will seek to maximise the income from an individual they control and this will often mean switching from one form of abuse to another or running more than one form of exploitation concurrently with another. For example, someone might be put to work on a farm but also be made to open a bank account to be used for laundering money. A woman may be forced to work in a brothel until she is heavily pregnant when she is then sent to do factory work. A child may be used as a domestic servant until he or she is of an age when they can be successfully put to work in a brothel or in an escort agency. On receipt of a female individual trafficked to them for factory work, a crime gang might decide, based on her looks and youth, instead, to sell her on to a brothel.

In a similar vein the trafficking or slavery experience may not be continuous or lifelong but just an episode in one or more migration or work experiences.

The enslavement may be time-limited until a person, for instance, repays a debt, serves out their debt bondage, or their usefulness in a particular field becomes redundant through age, fading looks, injury, pregnancy, illness or police interest.

Of course once the impediment has been overcome they may be re-trafficked or enslaved again.

When looking for trafficking or slavery we need to think and look at things as innovatively as possible, keep abreast of trends as we see them and never underestimate the depths to which some perpetrators will sink in their pursuit of profit.

In the next chapter we will look more closely at the nature of the victims being exploited. Issues of gender, age, nationality and culture will be explored together with, perhaps, more importantly, the effect that being trafficked or enslaved has upon their physical, mental and emotional well-being.

# CHAPTER SIX

## Who are the victims and how are they affected?

### Vera's story

Vera is thirty-nine and was born in Ukraine. When she was about seventeen years old she met an older man whom she married in Belarus. They divorced and Vera returned to Ukraine where she met her second husband. Although they married in a mosque, Vera did not want to become a Muslim but accompanied him to Lebanon anyway. She gave birth to a daughter in 2005. Her husband became gradually stricter and increasingly restrictive. Vera was very unhappy and one day, during a visit to the UK, when he went to see friends, she ran away with her daughter and claimed asylum. Her asylum claim was refused.

Following a complex sequence of events Vera returned to Ukraine from where her whole family had fled – her mother to Russia. Vera did not have many connections and had been in Lebanon for twelve years with her abusive partner. This experience of domestic violence made her especially vulnerable.

One day three armed men forced entry into her house. They beat Vera and told her she must go with them or they would hurt her daughter and her aunt. She was taken, bound, to different properties over the next week.

About two weeks later, she was forced into a lorry with five other women and taken to Istanbul where she was forced into prostitution and held against her will after being raped, beaten and abused by multiple men. Guards and heavy surveillance prevented her escape.

In 2017 a Turkish man in his fifties became fond of her. She saw him several times and spoke to him about her daughter whom she missed very much. He offered to let her use his phone to call her family. A few days later the same man came to see Vera and offered to help her escape. He bribed the security guard to let Vera go with him. He took her straight to his house and asked her to have sex with him to say thank you for his help. She agreed as she felt she had no other choice. He then offered to get her back to Ukraine.

Relieved to be reunited with her daughter and away from traumatic events, Vera felt unsafe living in Ukraine. Her whole family had scattered to different countries. Her aunt and uncle helped her raise funds to be smuggled into the UK.

"Josephine Bakhita, the saint originally from the Darfur region in Sudan, was kidnapped by slave-traffickers and sold to brutal masters when she was nine years old. Subsequently – as a result of painful experiences – she became a 'free daughter of God' thanks to her faith, lived in religious consecration and in service to others, especially the most lowly and helpless. This saint, who lived at the turn of the twentieth century, is even today an exemplary witness of hope for the many victims of slavery; she can support the efforts of all those committed to fighting against this 'open wound on the body of contemporary society, a scourge upon the body of Christ'".

*Pope Francis, Message for the World Day of Peace, 1 January 2015*

## The numbers

In 2017, the International Labour Office (ILO) and the Walk Free Foundation collaboratively compiled the global estimates of modern slavery. They reported that modern slavery covered a range of situations such as forced labour, debt bondage, forced marriage, other slavery and slavery-like practices, and human trafficking.

# In summary, the report found that on any given day in 2016:

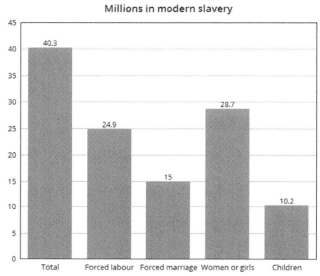

**Millions in modern slavery**

*ILO, Walk Free Foundation*

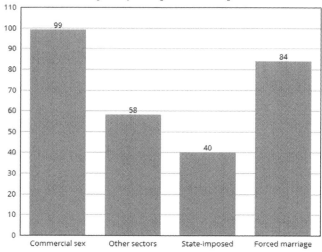

**29 million women and girls in forced labour**
Figures in percentages of total for all genders

*ILO, Walk Free Foundation*

## Is modern slavery regionalised?

Modern slavery occurs in every region of the world.

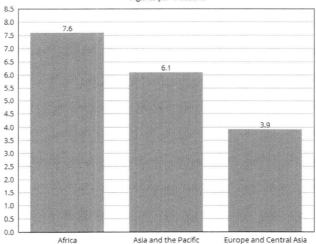

Regionalised slavery
Figures per thousand

*ILO, Walk Free Foundation*

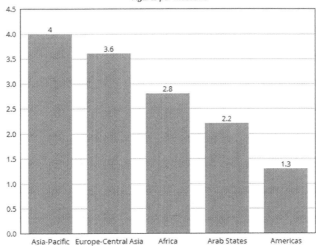

Forced labour
Figures per thousand

*ILO, Walk Free Foundation*

In the Arab States and the Americas, such data could be interpreted differently or liable to error. Hence their non-inclusion in the table showing regionalised slavery.

There is no "sameness" in the way the regions are affected by modern slavery. The accuracy of the statistics also depends on the data and whether or not Governments consider the data important.

## Is modern slavery industry specific?

The biggest proportion of adults who were in forced labour were domestic workers, followed by the construction industry, manufacturing, agriculture and fishing sectors.

An estimated 3.8 million adults were victims of forced sexual exploitation and one million children were victims of commercial sexual exploitation.

Other victims are victims of forced labour imposed by State authorities.

## Child labour

Worldwide, 218 million children between the ages of 5 and 17 years are in employment. Of these,

- 152 million children (10 per cent of the world's child population) are engaged in child labour.
  In 2016 this meant:
  - boys – 88 million
  - girls – 64 million
  - 5-11 years old – 73 million
  - 12-14 years old – 42 million
  - 15-17 years old – 37 million
  - primarily working in agriculture, which includes fishing, forestry, livestock herding and aquaculture, and relates to both subsistence and commercial farming
  - 23 per cent – self-employed (doubled since 2012)

- 73 million children (5 per cent of the world's children) work in hazardous conditions.
  - 15-17 years old – most prevalent age group
  - Under-12s – 19 million engaged in hazardous work

The ILO, Walk Free Foundation joint report indicated a decrease in child labour between 2000 and 2016. However it highlighted some concerns:

- increased child labour in Africa despite strong action to combat the problem
- 2012 to 2016 progress
  - partly attributable to broader labour market conditions and therefore possibly fragile
  - complicated by worldwide youth unemployment crisis: difficult for children above the minimum working age to find jobs
  - primarily limited to adolescents between 15-17 years old
  - virtually unchanged amongst children between 5-11 years old
- very little changed in the numbers of children engaged inforced labour, commercial sexual exploitation and other sectors of the private economy
- very difficult to identify and target child victims of forced labour

About half of those in child labour are unpaid, contributing, family workers in Africa's agricultural sector. This may be because of the high proportion of the population necessarily engaged in agriculture.

## Child labour victims by age
### Figures in millions

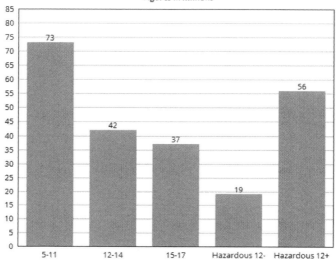

*ILO, Walk Free Foundation*

## Child labour victims by gender
### Figures in millions

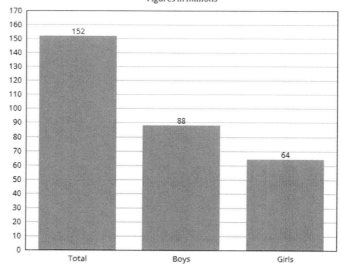

*ILO, Walk Free Foundation*

## Child labour victims by employment
### Figures in percentages

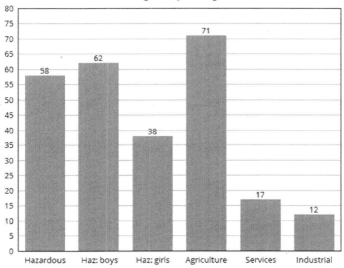

*Girl victims of child labour may be under-reported,*
*especially regarding domestic child labour.*
*ILO, Walk Free Foundation*

## Spot the difference

"I started working in the pottery at about the age of seven. I was allowed to make lids because it didn't matter too much if I broke one. I was gradually introduced into making increasingly complex items. This vase, for instance, takes about two months to make, working for a few hours each day. I am now forty-five, but it has taken me all these years to learn the necessary skills. Yes, making lids when I was seven wasn't much fun but I wouldn't be where I am today if it had been any different. My father, grandfather and great-grandfather also grew up in the pottery. I am training my son in the same way that they taught me. I don't think that any adult could 'just come in' and make one of these vases: it takes a lifetime to 'know' clay and its possibilities."

*Manuel, Master Potter, Toledo*


"I am at my workbench at dawn. I spend until evening doing fine embroidery that an adult's fingers are too big to manage. At midday the children are allowed into the yard for a short break and something to eat, but we are quickly sent back to our workbenches until sunset. My mother has food ready for me when I reach our home but I'm often too tired to eat. She doesn't want me to go out to work but I have three brothers and sisters and my father can only get occasional casual jobs. My family depends on the few rupees that I earn."

*Rahul, New Delhi*

In 2016, more than two-thirds of child labourers were family workers. In many developing countries, the difference between a family having food or going hungry might depend on whether or not the children can accompany their parents into the workplace. Not all child labour is enslavement. Similarly, where a trade is passed on from parent to child, such as agriculture, pottery and other crafts, the skill might take a lifetime to acquire.

## Men as victims

Men are also trafficked for sex. Their difficulty is that they are often too ashamed and embarrassed to talk about their inability to take care of themselves. Because of their feelings of shame, it is much harder to rescue and support male sex slaves.

## The UK situation

We do not have a full picture of what is happening. The last official Home Office report on numbers in 2014 calculated a possible 13,000 slaves in the UK but this is generally thought to be a very low estimate. As a snapshot of what the picture might look like these are some of the key points from the annual statistics for 2017 published by the National Crime Agency:

- 5,145 potential victims were submitted to the National Referral Mechanism in 2017 (a thirty-five per cent increase on 2016).
- Potential victims came from 116 different nationalities in 2017.
- Albanian, UK and Vietnamese nationals remained the most commonly reported potential victims.
- The most common exploitation type recorded for potential victims exploited as adults and children was labour exploitation, which also includes criminal exploitation.
- Child exploitation referrals in the UK increased by sixty-six per cent to 2,118 in 2017, compared to 1,278 in 2016.

## UK nationals

A significant number of "white British" are trafficked for labour and sexual exploitation. Recent cases of child exploitation in places such as such as Telford, Rochdale, Newcastle, Oxford and Rotherham are prime examples.

## The nature of the victims

Making generalisations about the victims is a waste of time and energy – and doesn't help them. There are, however, some commonly encountered factors.

## Vulnerable communities

Around the globe vulnerable communities offer fertile hunting grounds for traffickers and slave masters. These include
- refugees and migrants
- people fleeing war in the Middle East or famine in Africa

All too often a story of migration becomes one of the trafficking and exploitation of disenfranchised, unprotected and often unrecorded individuals at their most vulnerable. Traffickers use chaotic and badly policed situations to make money out of human suffering.

Domestic grooming for sexual exploitation happens in some of our larger UK cities. Some of the vulnerabilities that exist in individuals or in communities of individuals that have been seen to be exploited include:
- learning disabilities
- substance misuse
- youth
- poverty
- relationship breakdowns
- unemployment
- poor education
- homelessness
- illegal or irregular immigration status
- ethnicity

## Ethnic minorities

Certain ethnicities, classes or groups of people are over-represented in the exploited populations. Two such groups are:

- the Roma: This cultural group which spreads across Eastern Europe, with significant communities in Romania, Bulgaria, Albania and Slovakia, figures extremely heavily in any demographic study of victims. More often their low status and ill-treatment in their own country makes them an easy source of "stock" for the modern slavers from both within and without the Roma community itself.
- Dalits: In India and other parts of South Asia a formal, institutionalised caste system systemically disadvantages certain groups from birth. Amongst these the Dalits, scheduled castes or "untouchables", form the lowest structure of society and are subject to routine discrimination and exploitation by "higher" castes.

Leading on from this discussion of vulnerable communities and ethnic minorities we may also frame an exploration of the nature of victims in terms of "push" and "pull" factors.

## Push and pull factors

What factors create the situations for enslavement or trafficking?

### Push factors

- poverty
- unemployment
- war, famine and disease
- persecution, prejudice and discrimination
- coercion or physical force used by traffickers

### Pull factors

- the perception of Western Europe as a land of opportunity and wealth
- the deceptive promises of traffickers
- the West's demand for cheap labour and cheap goods
- the West's liberal attitude to prostitution and vice

- familial or community ties to overseas diasporas
- weak policing and frontier controls

## Patrick's story

Patrick was born and grew up in Northern Ireland. Through his heavy drinking, he lost his job and then his flat. Friendless, homeless and rough-sleeping, local travellers recruited him, offering Patrick well-paid work and somewhere to live.

Patrick was put to work laying drives and was paid in beer for doing work that he knew people did not need doing. He and others were given at least ten cans of beer a day. The travellers recruited non-English speaking workers and used Patrick to assess their standard of work. If he said a worker was no good then they were let go. Hard workers were kept on.

He stayed with the travellers for more than eight years. As he became more trusted, they would sometimes send him to the shop, demanding he return within a certain time. Patrick twice tried to escape but found he had no idea where to go. On his return to the site, he was beaten for being gone for too long. On the third escape attempt, the police found him, dishevelled, confused and wandering in a public place.

Patrick was initially admitted to a psychiatric ward for alcohol detox and treatment of his depression.

> In the first few days of being in the Medaille Trust safe house he was very traumatised and kept talking about going back to the travellers as he did not know what to do. However, with staff support, he began to feel safe. Patrick was helped to come to terms with his enslavement experience and to work towards independent living.

## The effect on victims

Not everyone reacts in the same way. Nobody comes through the damaging experience of enslavement without some lasting effects.

## Physical effects

Some of the most common things seen are:

- evidence of beatings and the use of physical force by traffickers
- evidence of untreated historical injuries such as fractures
- signs of work-related injuries (often from poor or non-existent health and safety practices)
- work-related diseases such as asbestosis or repetitive strain injury (RSI)
- malnutrition
- amongst those who have been sexually exploited – sexually transmitted infections (STIs), pelvic  inflammatory disease (PID), hepatitis and HIV/Aids
- In some countries such as the USA (and occasionally seen in the UK) a trafficker or pimp might brand or tattoo a sex worker.
- poor hygiene,  poor dental care and a need for glasses

## Psychological and mental health effects

Victims are likely to suffer from some form of mental health or psychological issue.

Is there a cause and effect situation? Was the original vulnerability exploited? Did the psychological effects come from the trauma of the person's trafficking or slavery experience?

Some of the most common conditions are:

- depression
- bi-polar states
- anxiety
- panic attacks
- insomnia
- stress
- Post-traumatic stress disorder (PTSD) This is a complex area with a wide range of signs and symptoms, a variety of treatments and a degree of uncertainty about prognoses. However, some commonly seen aspects of this debilitating condition are sleep disturbance, numbing, heightened sensitivities, flashbacks, forgetfulness, anger, rage, guilt, self-blame and extreme stress.
- substance misuse – This can be an existing addiction to drugs or alcohol that has been exploited to recruit or control the victim or induced to ensure compliance after the event.
- learning difficulties – often a pre-existing condition that have presented a vulnerability which the criminals have exploited

## Emotional effects

The emotional effects created by the trauma of being trafficked or enslaved can be enormous and are, of course, intimately linked to some of the mental health issues illustrated above. Emotional issues can include:

- low self-esteem
- low self-confidence
- a sense of disempowerment
- a sense of fearfulness

- "learned helplessness" through
  - exposure to large amounts of alcohol or drugs
  - isolation
  - food and sleep deprivation
  - disempowerment through violence and repeated rape
- guilt and self-blame , a feeling that "I deserve this"
- stigmatisation – particularly if the exploitation has been sexual
- Stockholm Syndrome

## Long-term or lasting damage

The ultimate objective of a trafficker or slaver is to turn another human being into a compliant money-earning slave. To do this, perpetrators employ tactics that can lead to long-term, and at times chronic or permanent, damage to an individual. Many of the physical effects illustrated above can be corrected by timely and appropriate clinical interventions by medical staff. The mental health and emotional issues can represent much more challenging and intractable problems for care staff and clinicians. Sadly, some consequences can last a lifetime.

# CHAPTER SEVEN

## Who are the perpetrators and how do they operate?

> "Our world demands of all government leaders a will which is effective, practical and constant, concrete steps and immediate measures for preserving and improving the natural environment and thus putting an end as quickly as possible to the phenomenon of social and economic exclusion, with its baneful consequences: human trafficking, the marketing of human organs and tissues, the sexual exploitation of boys and girls, slave labour, including prostitution, the drug and weapons trade, terrorism and international organised crime."
>
> *Pope Francis, Message to participants in the conference on human trafficking organised by the Santa Marta Group, Madrid, 30 October 2015*

## Introduction

It should be remembered that due to the nature of this and other criminal enterprises, our understanding of the situation must always be somewhat limited and so the examples given are illustrative and there is no attempt at comprehensiveness.

It is also important to note that Britain is not besieged by aggressive foreign criminals. The vast majority of minority ethnicities resident in the UK are not involved in this business. Also there is a certain amount of white British involvement in the trade.

## The perpetrators

"I saw him almost daily for almost four years. His English was only slightly better than my Italian, but he was always friendly and we chatted within the limits of our knowledge of each other's language. I was stunned when I discovered that he was a leading member of Rome's Mafia. I'd never have known. What crimes had he committed? I'd been completely taken in by his friendliness. How many others had he also fooled? I was never in any danger but after discovering his Mafia association, I could see that perhaps he could be very dangerous indeed. I was very careful not to change my behaviour towards him so we stayed on good terms throughout the four years."

*Joan*

## State-sponsored trafficking and slavery

"They had a 'Food for work' programme which employed women, knowing that the men would drink away any money or would sell the food to pay for alcohol. They knew that these mothers and grandmothers worked to feed their families. It really upset me to see the women mending the city's roads and culverts, work that a strong man would find exhausting. I'd daily see elderly grandmothers wielding pickaxes and pushing heavy wheelbarrows, watched by laughing, unemployed youths. All of that in exchange for a sack of maize flour and some cooking oil or beans... The work supervisor was a young woman, an expatriate, who did nothing, as far as I could see, to help those whom she guarded. The women were paid in food, but it was slave labour. In no way did the amount of food compensate their work."

*Sr Janet*

Although they are few and far between, there still exist examples of state-organised, sponsored or tolerated human trafficking and slavery around the world.

Perhaps the most obvious and most extreme example is the actions of North Korea. It provides significant numbers of manual labourers to a variety of commercial projects, largely concerning agriculture or construction, around the world, particularly in Asia and Africa.

The workers are "conscripted" through the Communist State's bureaucratic mechanisms and provided to client companies or governments as turnkey work forces; the remuneration for this goes

100

into the accounts of the State or individuals and the North Korean workers are never paid. The length of service on a project can often be several years.

A similar example is of the system of "military" conscription in Eritrea. Young men and women in Eritrea are, ostensibly, liable for conscription into the armed services as in many other countries. Eritrea, however, uses the system as a thinly veiled form of State slavery. The "conscripts" are not paid, live in appalling conditions and their length of service is unlimited. Only a few of those conscripted serve in formed military units as we would understand them. The remainder are employed in serving on State construction, infrastructure or agricultural projects according to the Government's needs. Significant numbers of this youthful group are also used in agriculture or simply as cost-free labour by the warlords and oligarchs who control the failing, rogue state.

In Libya, officials take advantage of the domestic breakdown of law and order and of Libya's position as the main thoroughfare for migration from Central and Western Africa to Europe. Unscrupulous gangs prey on the vulnerabilities of those transiting the country. Extortion, blackmail, brutality and exploitation characterise the heavily armed gangs trading throughout the country in human beings. There is substantial evidence, including videos, of the open auctioning and sale of slaves, both male and female, to the highest bidder.

Slavery, as a deeply ingrained, institutionalised cultural practice, has long been practised in Mauritania. Recent extensive anti-slavery laws have been passed by the Government after pressure from the UN and the EU. However, they are not enforced and the widespread and relatively open nature of slavery in the country indicates a degree of Government collusion, if not sponsorship.

Other examples include the trafficking of individuals in Somalia and the widespread use of child soldiers in Africa and Asia, all of which show the hand of the State, or what passes for the State, in their operation.

Other cases of state sponsorship or collusion may be more subtle or nuanced.

## "Cultural" trafficking and slavery

In some countries, slavery is a deeply ingrained cultural practice: children are often born into slavery. The fact that a practice may be described as cultural, traditional or endemic does not of course justify its perpetuation or tolerance but it does add a layer of complexity and difficulty in discussing, letting alone dealing with the problem.

The human rights violations perpetrated through trafficking and slavery can never be excused by references to culture, race, historical convention or tradition.

### Look deeper

"Can't people see that I am more than just the woman who cleans their toilets? I taught literature before I was captured. I cope with my work by reciting poetry to myself."

*Natalya*

Trafficking into the UK was for a long period considered the work of "outsiders" or foreign nationals. However, over recent years it has become apparent that, in many cases, the diasporas of other countries resident in the UK are playing a significant role in trafficking and receiving slaves. These diasporas have in some cases been embedded in the UK for generations and contain many dual nationals. Unfortunately they are just as likely or unlikely to contain criminal elements as any other groups of individuals.

Diaspora connections have figured prominently in many cases of trafficking and slavery. These deviant groups within immigrant communities can act as middlemen or -women, creating bridging networks between the sending country and the UK.

In addition, we are increasingly seeing criminal groups who operate solely in the UK within their diaspora, preying on citizens from their own home ethnic grouping. For example, in order to reduce the risks involved in moving people about in Europe, perpetrators in the UK often "recruit" from the population of their nationals already resident in the UK. A group of Romanian victims rescued from a farm in Lincolnshire were as likely to have been trafficked from Sheffield as from Bucharest.

## Organised crime groups (OCGs)

The role of Organised Crime Groups or OCGs in trafficking and slavery is perhaps the best known or most familiar example of how this crime operates. Certainly such groups are key players in the trade and account for much of the misery that ensues.

In his book *McMafia*, Misha Glenny gives a good account of how modern OCGs tend to operate. The traditional Sicilian Mafia, the Cosa Nostra, have little history of involvement with prostitution and trafficking. However, other Italian-based OCGs such as the Campanian Camorra or the Calabrian based 'Ndrangheta have proved less squeamish, as have the OCGs based on the Italian-Nigerian or Italian-Arab diasporas with whom they often work in partnership, as described earlier.

After the fall of communism in Eastern Europe in the early 1990s an alarming number of OCGs appeared in a number of countries. Exploiting the collapse of the totalitarian regimes and aided by a twisted view of what capitalism had to offer, these OCGs quickly spotted the potential profit from trading in human beings.

In general terms OCGs will seek activities that are low-risk and high return. Human trafficking is certainly a high return operation as an enslaved individual can be sold many times and continues to generate profit for his or her controller, unlike drugs or arms that can only be sold once.

In the chaos resulting from the fall of the Russian hegemony of Eastern Europe the risks incumbent in trading in human beings were low. Other factors later allowed the trade to flourish:

- The Balkan Wars created more lawlessness and anarchy.
- Free movement in the Schengen Zone of the European Union continued the low-risk operating environment.
- a general lack of awareness amongst the public and law enforcement agencies
- Amongst the European Mafia-like groups, some nationalities in particular have established significant criminal empires, noted for their violence.

Eastern European OCGs are not however the only threat posed. Other example of OCGs can be found amongst the Triads originating from China, Taiwan, Hong Kong and Macau such as the 14K or WSW both of which have presences in the UK. Originally formed as secret societies dedicated to resisting Western expansion in China, they now operate almost entirely as criminal gangs with a global influence and spread as Chinese communities have been established overseas. Active gangs of Triads exist in the UK, Canada, Australia, Malaysia, South Korea and the USA as well as many European countries. Their influence over prostitution and trafficking, in many countries, is significant.

Other OCGs are emerging from countries such as Nigeria and Vietnam as groups of criminally-minded individuals come together in search of the quick profits that can be made from trading in human misery.

In Vietnam OCGs appear to have links to the military. In some countries, the cultural acceptance of corruption assists in creating a low-risk environment in which to operate.

Corruption inevitably plays a part in the success of any OCG and the more successful groups operate out of countries where a degree of tolerance if not cooperation is exercised by the State.

## A family business?

The Mafia-like OCGs described above are often seen or described as "families" and it is useful at times to see trafficking and slavery as a family activity. True, it is a step down from a true OCG with its hierarchical structures and codes of behaviour, and has much more in common with a "cottage industry", engaged in by entrepreneurs of a criminal disposition and low or non-existent moral standards. In such situations:

- human trafficking and slavery is seen as a means of making easy money
- social networks provide information and support
- "tradecraft" is passed on by word of mouth
- trafficking and slavery
  - may be sustained or a one-off episode
  - are less formal and structured than an OCG
  - can appear and disappear at short notice
  - can paradoxically be either a very easy or a very difficult target for law enforcement agencies
  - might be the building block for larger criminal enterprise
  - may specialise in a particular aspect of the trafficking trade

## Domestic trafficking

The UK has a significant problem with domestic, internal trafficking and some examples of this are explored below.

### Travellers

Another important group involved in trafficking and slavery are, unfortunately, the traveller community resident in the UK.

Although only a small minority is involved in trafficking, its frequency within the community means that it can no longer be seen as atypical.

High profile cases have seen some family members prosecuted with several individuals receiving heavy sentences of many years in jail.

The victims of these families are often UK nationals or East Europeans, almost always male and often drawn from itinerant or homeless communities. Forced to live on traveller sites in sheds, stables or derelict caravans, poorly fed and denied access to basic hygiene and sanitation facilities, these individuals receive little or no remuneration for the work they do.

The victims tend to be forced to work on traditional traveller trading activities such as scrap metal collecting, tarmacking and small-scale building works.

Forced criminality is common, with victims required to carry out robberies or burglaries, be part of scams and confidence tricks or assist in demanding money with menaces.

### Grooming gangs

In recent years there has been increasing, distressing, evidence of groups of male UK citizens in urban conurbations, small and large, such as Rotherham, Oxford, Newcastle and Bradford coming together to form gangs that groom young women for sexual exploitation.

Those involved prey on girls with existing vulnerabilities and needs particularly those in the care of the Social Services. Many of these girls are young adults or children and the grooming can begin as early as age twelve or thirteen.

Once a girl has been groomed, perhaps using some of the "lover boy" techniques outlined earlier, she becomes the "property" of the group and is passed around the group for abuse or provided to those outside of the group for money as a form of enforced prostitution. Such girls are often fed alcohol and drugs as a means of control.

### The UK as an exporting country

It is increasingly evident that the UK is not only a destination and transit country for victims of trafficking and slavery but is also a source country.

Our knowledge of the trade or export of human beings from the UK is, at present, only sketchy but the following "tips of the icebergs" of movement have been noted:

- female UK nationals from the UK to other EU countries for the purposes of sexual exploitation. The biographical work of Sophie Hayes, *Trafficked*, gives a good description of this type of trade.
- male UK nationals by traveller groups to Scandinavia for the purposes of labour exploitation
- female UK nationals from Asian diasporas to "home" countries for the purposes of forced marriages
- UK females to Japan for the purposes of sexual exploitation
- UK nationals coerced or encouraged to go abroad for the purposes of the removal and sale of organs, particularly in South Asia

The above examples only reflect what we know at the moment; there is undoubtedly, and sadly, more to be uncovered as our knowledge of slavery increases.

### Individuals

Another phenomenon we are beginning to understand is the role an individual can play in trafficking or slavery, purchasing a single slave for "personal" use for:

- forced marriage
- domestic service
- exercising power and control over

A one-off fee is paid to the traffickers or a middleman and the slave is delivered to the purchaser. Although the purchaser or "owner" takes no part in the movement of the individual, their continued "ownership" and control of the victim is as criminal an act as anyone else's.

## How the criminals operate

How the criminal gangs, groupings and individuals work is a complicated and often intricate subject, heavily contextualised as to the type of trafficking, the victims being exploited and the countries of origin, transit and destination. However, some general points may be made and, for ease of understanding, the process has been split into three components: procurement, transportation and control.

## Procurement

The direct use of force, violence or intimidation against a victim, often, in extreme cases, including abduction, is still occasionally seen but is far less common than most people would perhaps think. Nevertheless, actual or threatened harm to an individual, their family or associates remains a technique amongst certain groups of traffickers.

More commonly seen however are other, more subtle, forms of deception or coercion used to ensnare or entrap individuals.

A primary example of this is the use of debt bondage. A debt is created between the victim and the trafficker – perhaps in respect of the travel costs of the move or as a fee for securing employment in a foreign country.

Once the debt has been created the victim is then in the power of the traffickers. Such power can then be used not only to ensure the move within or to another country takes place but also to maintain future control over the victim.

Of course such debts can be increased by further charges for accommodation or interest in such a manner that the debt becomes unmanageable and is never paid off.

Another significant method of recruitment of victims is the use of grooming or "lover boy" tactics. Here an individual will seek to gain the confidence of the victim by, perhaps, presenting as a boyfriend who wants to start a new life in the UK and will eventually marry their victim. Similar techniques are used when perpetrators present themselves as friends or relatives interested, for altruistic reasons, in helping the victim obtain advancement or a better lifestyle.

In certain cultural contexts, the belief in witchcraft or magic can be used to aid recruitment (and later control) with individuals undergoing elaborate rituals as part of their recruitment or procurement.

These types of recruitment when combined with the full array of false job offers, fake recruitment agencies, Internet advertisements and idealised presentations of life and opportunities in the UK can prove irresistible to vulnerable men and women seeking to migrate or just to have a better life.

## Transportation

The preferred method used by traffickers to move a victim will be by legal or legitimate routes of transportation such as scheduled airlines and official visas to reduce the risk inherent in their operations. Only when these are not possible will they resort to clandestine forms of transportation such as smuggling an individual across a border in the back of a lorry or transporting an undocumented person by small boat.

As such we are as likely to see a victim arrive in the UK on a scheduled airline flight and in possession of, say, a correctly issued student or tourist visa and staying, initially, in a respectable hotel chain as we are to see them smuggled covertly through a border crossing point or port.

When these methods are not available, false papers or passports may be used. In all cases traffickers will look for airports or seaports where they believe security is weak or can be outwitted. The Channel Tunnel and the ports of Dover, Newhaven and Hull have historically fitted this description along with Heathrow, Gatwick and Stansted.

## Control

Many of the techniques and methods discussed earlier when we looked at procurement will run through a trafficking experience and be used to continue the control exerted over an individual during their horrific experiences.

As we have already seen, the creation of debt bondage is a good example of this. The continued use of threats of violence against the individual or familial connections is an obvious further method of control although subtler forms of emotional or psychological methods are commonly used:

- physical isolation from the wider community
- limited access to, and communication with the outside world
- removal of passports and ID
- enforced reliance on traffickers or slave masters for food and accommodation

- discouragement from learning English
- fabricated/fostered fear towards authorities:
    - claims of corruption
    - automatic jail sentence for presence in the UK
- threats of curses, misfortune arising from witchcraft or voodoo
- enforced reliance on "lover boy"

## Ancillary business and benefits

With the exception of a few rare instances, the perpetrators of these crimes are in it to pursue financial profit – they wish to make money from the human misery they create in order to satisfy their greed.

More likely than not, they will also be involved in other aspects of criminality such as drug-dealing, selling arms, peddling counterfeit goods, pornography or smuggling.

Individuals who limit their criminality solely to trafficking and slavery are rare.

They will see the individual they are trafficking or enslaving as an exploitable commodity. While the individual may produce cheap labour or sexual services for an OCG, they will also have an ancillary use as someone who:

- can open a bank account to facilitate money laundering
- has an identity that can be used to falsely claim benefits
- can recruit or coerce others when required

**References**

Glenny M (2008) *McMafia: A Journey Through the Criminal Underworld*, London: Penguin.

Hayes S (2012) *Trafficked: My Story*, London: Harper Collins.

# CHAPTER EIGHT

## Trafficking as a market place

"Dangerous conditions and threats of violence are faced by too many in the industry.

Imagine going to work every day with no contract, no rights and no guarantee of payment. Working in terrible, often dangerous conditions and sometimes forced to sleep on site. The days are long, with no breaks and the lingering threat of violence.

This is the reality for too many construction workers in the capital — a world of slavery in which they are trapped by the need to pay rent and the broken promises of men who pick them up in a van early each morning and drive them to their next job. Of course, these crimes are in no way typical of the industry — most of London's construction firms treat their employees fairly, but they can be let down by those who exploit fractured supply chains and high demand for labour.

In London, nationals from other EU countries account for twenty-seven per cent of the construction workforce.

The Met is working hard with partners to tackle the organised criminal networks at the heart of trafficking and slavery operations. At City Hall, we set up the London Modern Slavery Partnership Board to work with agencies including the

Met, Home Office, trade unions, NGOs and local authorities, sharing intelligence and pooling resources.

This way, we can target sites across London where slavery and labour exploitation are conducted in plain view — at street-based pick-up points for white vans, in the car parks of some trading estates and at small-scale refurbishments.

Many construction firms are themselves doing good work to prevent and eradicate abuse in their supply chains.

We're also working on developing industry standards that will build on the Mayor's Good Work Standard which will encourage businesses to promote best practice in employment. And we're raising awareness across relevant agencies and frontline staff to help everyone who may come into contact with people trapped in slavery – from housing officers to health and safety inspectors – feel confident about playing their part in fighting these crimes.

Forced labour in construction is a relatively new area for law enforcement to tackle. Awareness in the sector itself is growing, but it is still difficult to grasp the true scale of the problem. Only by working together will we be able to bring about change and improve the lives of those who are trapped and suffering."

*Sophie Linden, Deputy Mayor for Policing and Crime in London, writing in the Evening Standard, 2 December 2017*

## The market economics of modern slavery and human trafficking

"As I have often said, and now willingly reiterate, business is 'a noble vocation, directed to producing wealth and improving our world', especially 'if it sees the creation of jobs as an essential part of its service to the common good' (*Laudato Si'*, 129). As such, it has a responsibility to help overcome the complex crisis of society and the environment, and to fight poverty. This will make it possible to improve the precarious living conditions of millions of people and bridge the social gap which gives rise to numerous injustices and erodes fundamental values of society, including equality, justice and solidarity."

*Pope Francis, Message to the Executive President of the World Economic Forum, Davos-Klosters, 30 December 2015*

### Annual profits from slavery and trafficking (ILO 2017)

- Total profit: US$ 150 billion (£113 billion)
- US$ 34 billion (£25.6 billion) through construction, manufacturing, mining and utilities
- US$ 9 billion (£6.8 billion) through agriculture, including forestry and fishing
- US$ 8 billion (£6 billion) saved by private households by not paying or underpaying domestic workers held in forced labour

The ILO estimate indicates that:
- more than half of the people in forced labour are women and girls, primarily in commercial sexual exploitation and domestic work
- men and boys are primarily in forced economic exploitation in agriculture, construction and mining

At a simplistic level, traffickers fulfil a demand from several global sources:
- employers (employers, owners, managers or sub-contractors) in various industries
- consumer-demand clients (in the sex industry)
- corporate buyers (in manufacturing)
- household members (in domestic work)
- third parties involved in the process (recruiters, agents, transporters and others who participate knowingly in the movement of persons for the purposes of exploitation)
- transporters of those fleeing economic or conflict situations

"Weeping for other people's pain does not only mean sharing in their sufferings, but also and above all, realising that our own actions are a cause of injustice and inequality. Let us open our eyes, then, and see the misery of the world, the wounds of our brothers and sisters who are denied their dignity, and let us recognize that we are compelled to heed their cry for help! May we reach out to them and support them so they can feel the warmth of our presence, our friendship, and our fraternity! May their cry become our own, and together may we break down the barriers of indifference that too often reign supreme and mask our hypocrisy and egoism!'"

*Pope Francis, Message to the Executive President of the World Economic Forum, Davos-Klosters, 30 December 2015*

## Where is modern trafficking seen?

"The supply of contemporary trafficked slaves is promoted by long-standing factors such as poverty, lawlessness, social instability, military conflict, environmental disaster, corruption and acute bias against female gender and minority ethnicities."

*Siddharth Kara, Harvard International Review*
*12 April 2016*

Modern trafficking is seen in numerous situations and more visibility and awareness has been raised in relation to the following sectors:

- farms and meat processing
- cannabis farming
- nail bars
- car washes
- brothels, massage parlours and saunas
- the street sex trade
- corporate responsibility
- supply chains
- business

## Why and how?

Why does trafficking occur and why is it more prevalent in certain countries than others?

There are several factors underpinning the existence of trafficking:

- the poverty cycle
- increased demand for cheap labour
- increased demand for cheaper material goods
- pressures of business competition (although there are legal frameworks obliging businesses to look at this and eliminate slavery within its supply)
- lack of education, illiteracy, gender and migration

Whilst there are movements to address the issue, in certain countries or industries trafficking and enslavement continue because:

- little or no unionisation means that workers
  - do not always know of their entitlements
  - do not have employee rights
  - lack the processes to raise complaints about work conditions, pay and labour
  - must pay recruiters high recruitment charges
- unregulated sectors allow employers to avoid providing
  - workers' rights
  - sanitary work conditions
  - compensation in the event of employee injury or death
- in the absence of appropriate health and safety legislation
  - workers do not feature in governments' annual reports on occupational deaths
  - the extent of occupational deaths is not public knowledge
  - there is little incentive to improve legislation
  - the greatest impact might be on minority communities regarded as undeserving of legislative focus (for example, Dalit communities in India)

# CHAPTER NINE

## Spotting the signs and what you should do

"Certainly there is a lot of ignorance on the topic of trafficking. But sometimes there also seems to be little will to understand the scope of the issue. Why? Because it touches close to our conscience; because it is thorny; because it is shameful. Then there are those who, even knowing this, do not want to speak because they are at the end of the 'supply chain', as a user of the 'services' that are offered on the street or on the Internet. There are, lastly, those who do not want it to be talked about, because they are directly involved in the criminal organisations that reap handsome profits from trafficking. Yes, it takes courage and honesty, when, in our daily lives, we meet or deal with persons who could be victims of human trafficking, or when we are tempted to select items which may well have been produced by exploiting others.

The work of raising awareness must begin at home, with ourselves, because only in this way will we be able to then make our communities aware, motivating them to commit themselves so that no human being may ever again be a victim of trafficking."

*Pope Francis, Address to participants in the World Day of Prayer, Reflection and Action against Human Trafficking, 12 February 2018*

## Introduction

The crimes of trafficking and slavery are both, paradoxically, hidden away from the public yet also in plain sight.

With few exceptions these are crimes undertaken by criminals to gain profit. As such, they

- provide a product or service to the public or a subset of the public
- must advertise or attract customers
- require some form of contact or encounter with the public
- generate indicators and signs of trafficking should cause concern and which
  - the general public can recognise
  - can help to identify local community situations of trafficking and slavery
  - must be reported to law enforcement agencies or other statutory bodies

Don't forget, however, that some signs will be invisible to the "ordinary" observer, who would be unlikely to know about a nail bar worker's living conditions, pay, or have access to personal documents.

This Chapter lists some indicators and signs of trafficking that should generate concern if noticed. None of these lists is exhaustive.

## Spot the signs of exploitation

A good place to begin looking at the signs and indicators of trafficking may be with the Government's own National Referral Mechanisms (NRM). Agencies wishing to refer victim's or potential victims into the NRM are invited to go through some check lists to indicate if a particular sign or indicator is present. These lists are grouped according to the type of exploitation and are reproduced below: none is exhaustive. They are the basis on which law enforcement agencies begin the process of identifying victims and investigating the crimes.

There are many other sources of further advice and help available to those agencies and to the general public.

## Indicators of domestic servitude occurring wholly or partly within residential premises

- living with and working for a family in a private home or place of accommodation
- not eating with the rest of the family or being given only leftovers or inadequate food
- no private sleeping place or sleeping in shared space, for example, in the living room
- no private space
- forced to work in excess of normal working hours or being "on call" twenty-four hours per day
- never leaving the house without permission from the employer
- in case of escape, employer
  - reports them as a "missing person"
  - alleges theft or other crime related to the escape

## Indicators of forced or compulsory labour

- no or limited access to earnings or labour contract
- excessive wage reductions, withheld wages or financial penalties
- depends on employer for services such as work, transport and accommodation
- must pay for tools, food or accommodation via imposed deductions from their received pay
- imposed place of accommodation
- found in poor living conditions
- evidence of excessive working days or hours
- deceived about the nature of the job, location, or employer
- employer or manager unable to produce
  - documents required when employing migrant labour
  - records of wages paid to workers
- poor or non-existent health and safety equipment or no health and safety notices
- any other evidence of labour laws being breached

## Indicators of sexual exploitation

- adverts for sexual services offering individuals from particular ethnic or national groups
- sleeping on work premises
- movement between brothels or working in alternate locations
- very limited clothing or a large proportion of "sexual" clothing
- only speaks sexual words in local language or language of client group
- tattoos or other marks indicating "ownership" by their exploiters
- force, intimidation or coercion into providing sexual services
- subjection to crimes such as abduction, assault or rape
- clients pay someone other than the potential victim
- health symptoms (including sexual health issues)

## General indicators for modern slavery

- distrust of authorities
- expression of fear or anxiety
- signs of psychological trauma (including post-traumatic stress disorder, PTSD)
- acts as if instructed by another
- injuries apparently a result of assault or controlling measures
- evidence of control over movement, either as an individual or as a group
- found in, or connected to, a type of location likely to be used for exploitation
- restricted movement and confinement to the workplace or to a limited area
- passport or documents held by someone else
- lack of access to medical care
- limited social contact/isolation
- limited contact with family
- signs of ritual abuse and witchcraft (juju)
- substance misuse
- forced, intimidated or coerced into providing services

- doesn't know home or work address
- perceived debt bondage
- enforced salary deductions for food or accommodation
- threatened with being handed over to authorities
- threats made against the individual or their family members
- forcibly placed in a dependency situation
- no or limited access to bathroom or hygiene facilities
- self-identifies

These lists are the basis on which law enforcement agencies begin the process of identifying victims and investigating the crimes. As we will see below, there also a myriad of further advice and help available to those agencies and to the general public.

## Non-NRM Lists of signs and indicators

As an example of the further advice and guidance available, we show below some further checklists. By the nature of these things there is some repetition.

## What to look for

Domestic servitude is quite prevalent globally but is not easy to identify. Certain factors that may indicate domestic servitude are, a person who may:

- live and work for a family in a private home
- not eat with the rest of the family
- have no bedroom or proper sleeping place
- have no private space
- be forced to work excessive hours; be "on call" twenty-four hours a day
- never leave the house without the "employer"
- be malnourished
- be reported as missing or accused of crime by their "employer" if they try to escape

## Warning signs

The warning signs of trafficking or modern slavery can be very subtle. People who have been trafficked may:

- show signs of consistent abuse or have untreated health issues
- have no identification documents in their personal possession, and little or no finances of their own
- be unwilling to talk without a more "senior" controlling person around, who may act as their translator
- sleep in a cramped, unhygienic room in a building that they are unable to freely leave
- be unable to leave their place of work to find different employment and fear that bad things may happen if they do
- be charged at an unrealistic and inflated rate for accommodation or transport as a condition of employment, costs which are deducted from wages

## Children

The lists shown earlier came from the NRM's adult referral form. Shown below are the checklists available from the National Society for the Prevention of Cruelty to Children (NSPCC) for considering cases of possible child trafficking or slavery.

## Signs that a child has been trafficked

Signs that a child has been trafficked may not be obvious but you might notice unusual behaviour or events. These include a child who:

- spends a lot of time doing household chores
- rarely leaves their house, has no freedom of movement and no time for playing
- is orphaned or living apart from their family, often in unregulated private foster care
- lives in substandard accommodation
- is not sure which country, city or town they're in
- is unable or reluctant to give details of accommodation or personal details

- might not be registered with a school or a GP practice
- has no documents or has falsified documents
- has no access to their parents or guardians
- is seen in inappropriate places such as brothels or factories
- possesses unaccounted money or goods
- is permanently deprived of a large part of their earnings, required to earn a minimum amount of money every day or pay off an exorbitant debt
- has injuries from workplace accidents
- gives a prepared story which resembles those given by other children

## Signs that an adult is involved in child trafficking

There are also signs that an adult is involved in child trafficking, such as:

- multiple visa applications for different children
- acting as a guarantor for multiple visa applications for children
- travelling with different children to whom they are unrelated or for whom they are not legally responsible
- insisting on remaining with, and speaking for, the child
- living with unrelated or newly-arrived children
- abandoning a child or claiming not to know a child previously in their company

## Specialist advice

There are many useful lists covering most possible situations of trafficking and/or modern slavery. The National Crime Agency (NCA), for example, offers the following indications to those working in the financial sector:

## Specialist advice

- European Economic Area (EEA) nationals opening accounts, based at houses of multiple occupancy
- EEA nationals who open accounts and

- are accompanied and assisted by a "translator" who also seems to control them
- appear confused, with poor or no English and may not know their address
- depend on the translator to
  - answer questions on their behalf
  - retain control of their documents
  - show them where to sign
  - fill in the forms or bring in a completed application form
- unusual and identifiable pattern or frequency of opening accounts
- wage payments which remain untouched for long periods even if from legitimate, often nationwide staff agencies
- unusual withdrawal patterns
- multiple accounts cleared out in succession at the same cash point
- receives funds from multiple payday loans companies, which are then withdrawn in one lump sum, sometimes to overseas accounts
- payments from the UK but cleared by a European Union (EU) country

## Benefit trafficking account indicators

- EEA nationals opening accounts whilst based in houses of multiple occupancy
- EEA nationals opening accounts in a branch with a "translator" assisting or appearing to control the victim (as above)
- accounts showing
  - unusual pattern or frequency of opening
  - receiving only benefit payments which then remain in the account with no regular spending withdrawals for activities such as food shopping
  - unusual withdrawal patterns
  - UK holding but EU clearance
- multiple accounts cleared out in quick succession at the same cash point

## Victim identity hijack indicators

In recent cases, victims recovered and returned to Eastern Europe were found to have been made company directors of a seven-figure GBP turnover company which is now under investigation for money laundering. Key factors were:

- company or business accounts in EEA national names
- regular account income
- account holders and directors
  - not seen running day-to-day transactions
  - difficult to meet
  - appear unaware of business activities
- multiple deposit-makers, often in cash, to a small number of payees

## Child trafficking and illegal adoption indicators

There are many different aspects of child trafficking and illegal adoption. Some criminals use informal fostering to source minors from the former overseas territories of EU countries. In these instances, minors were then exploited as domestic workers or in businesses. Key factors and pointers for these cases were:

- regular account income from payees in former EU country overseas territories
- increased overseas payments at the start of school terms
- frequently identified as males of secondary school age
- The payments are sent to the person in the UK who is arranging for the victim to be brought to the UK for illegal adoption and exploitation. In some cases payments of £10,000 have been made to arrange the illegal adoption.

## Become expert

Checklists like the ones shown above are extremely useful but, over time, experts from law enforcement agencies and NGOs need to gain further expertise more detailed knowledge. They need to know the local context and keep abreast of current trends in human trafficking and slavery. The example given in Chapter Five of *The Mystery of the Chewing Gum Thefts* is a good demonstration of how doing this can produce dividends.

However the check lists are good starting tools.

## What we should do

Of course being able to spot the signs and indicators of human trafficking and slavery is only part of the process. Spotting signs without reporting them is, potentially, leaving people in danger and in a situation of continuing exploitation. It is important to remember:

- Do not ignore any signs or indicators – report them.
- Report things swiftly – do not leave them to think about it or to confirm things.
- Do not assume someone else has reported it.
- Do not think it is too trivial to report.
- Do not think you will look foolish if you are wrong and it is not trafficking or slavery.
- Do not be tempted to carry out further investigations: that is the job of the police.

REPORT IT

If you think someone is in immediate danger,
please call the police on 999.

If you think someone is a potential victim but there is no
immediate threat to life, please call the local police on 101.

If you have information you wish to give anonymously and
confidentially you can call Crimestoppers on 0800 555 111.

REPORT IT

"One strategy which includes a greater awareness of the theme of trafficking, beginning with a clear terminology and with the concrete testimonies of protagonists, can certainly be of help. Real awareness about the topic, however, devotes attention to the 'demand for trafficking' that is behind the offer (chain of consumption); we are all called to reject hypocrisy and to face the idea of being part of the problem, rather than turn away proclaiming our innocence... Of course, arresting traffickers is an obligation of justice. But the true solution is the conversion of hearts, cutting off demand in order to dry out the market."

*Pope Francis, Address to participants in the World Day of Prayer, Reflection and Action against Human Trafficking, 12 February 2018*

# CHAPTER TEN
The response

## Introduction

While it is probably true to say that trafficking and slavery have always existed in the UK, we simply and fondly believed for many years that it had gone away. It was only in the late 1990s that there was a growing awareness that we were mistaken.

## The statutory response

Over time, the work of campaigning NGOs and some concerned Parliamentarians brought a deeper understanding of the issues related to human trafficking and a strident call for urgent action.

- 2006: creation of the United Kingdom Human Trafficking Centre
- 2009: introduction of the National Referral Mechanism (NRM)
- 2011: first victim support funding became widely available
- 2015: Modern Slavery Act (MSA 2015)

  Much has been achieved: much still remains to be done.

## Legislation

The Modern Slavery *Act* of 2015 sought to bring together all existing human trafficking and modern slavery legislation into one piece of law.

It introduced a variety of other measures such as the introduction of an Independent Anti-slavery Commissioner and some corporate responsibilities around transparency in supply chains. It was billed by Government as "ground-breaking" legislation that established the UK as the global leader in the fight against slavery. Inevitably, there have been some missed opportunities. Nevertheless, even the most scathing of critics is likely to admit that it is a step in the right direction.

## Law enforcement

Significant steps forward have been made in recent years amongst law enforcement communities:

- Most regional police forces train officers to proactively deal with occasions of trafficking and enslavement.
- Some police forces such as the Metropolitan Police and Greater Manchester Police have set up specialist units.
- A significant number of forces are engaged with local or regional Modern Slavery Partnerships that bring together law enforcement, statutory agencies and NGOs to jointly study and address the problem.
- The National Crime Agency runs the Modern Slavery Human Trafficking Unit, a successor to the United Kingdom Human Trafficking Centre.

## Other agencies

- Gangmasters and Labour Abuse Authority (GLAA)
- Her Majesty's Revenue and Customs (HMRC)
- the Health and Safety Executive
- local authority Housing, Trading Standards and Planning Departments
- immigration-related services, the Border Force and UK Visas and Immigration. These are gradually moving beyond their limited terms of illegal immigration.

## Prosecutions

Despite the enhanced provisions in the Modern Slavery Act 2015, sentences are often light.

The Crown Prosecution Service is working hard to address this and the steady, if slow, rise in the number of cases being successfully brought to court is expected to continue.

## Victim support

Since the introduction first of the National Referral Mechanism and more latterly of Government funding, services offering victim support have greatly improved.

A network of safe houses exists across the UK, ready and able to take victims as they are rescued or identified. At any one time 300-400 victims are in support of this nature with several hundred others being supported in the community by outreach services where it is safe to do so.

All of the services for adults are run by NGOs while the provision of support to minors remains a matter for local authority Social Services teams.

Adult services provide a variety of assistance and interventions including:
- housing
- subsistence payments
- clothing
- food
- medical care
- counselling
- employment advice
- immigration advice
- support through the criminal justice process

Such services undoubtedly need refining, improving and expanding but they are a far cry from the early days of no provision.

## Addressing demand – The Nordic Model

The Nordic Model was mentioned in Chapter 2 as a means of addressing sexual exploitation, but does it work?

As described earlier, this approach to prostitution (sometimes also known as the Sex Buyer Law, or the Swedish, Abolitionist, or Equality Model):

- decriminalises those who are prostituted
- provides support services to help them exit
- makes buying people for sex a criminal offence
- reduces the demand that drives sex trafficking
  The Nordic model has two main goals:
- to curb the demand for commercial sex that fuels sex trafficking
- the promote equality between men and women

Since the introduction of the law, it has been suggested that street prostitution has decreased and Sweden has become an undesirable destination for pimps and traffickers. (Chapter 4, Swedish Ministry of Justice, *English summary of the evaluation of the ban on purchase of sexual services (1999-2008)*, 2 July 2010) In addition, the new law has influenced attitudes regarding the purchase of sex: from 1996 (before the law) until 2008, the number of male sex buyers decreased from 13.6 per cent to 7.9 per cent.

However:

- differences between the Nordic countries mean that there is no shared "Nordic model"
- when sex workers are victims according to the law, they face even greater stigma when they are caught
- despite Sweden's protection of sex workers, there is often tension concerning
  - relationships with police and landlords
  - issues like child custody

France (2016):

- enacted similar legislation to the Swedish model
- treats the sex worker as a victim rather than a criminal
- allows foreign sex workers, many illegally in France, to acquire a temporary residence permit if they try to find other work

Cracking down on clients can

- push sex workers further underground
- transition sex working from the street to the Internet
- push sex workers into vulnerable situations with less protection

The UK, to date, has resisted introducing similar legislation. The question is whether the criminalisation of customers purchasing sex has reduced sex trafficking – again there is no conclusive answer to this. In Germany where prostitution is legalised and sex workers have allegedly better working conditions, studies have shown that exploitation and trafficking are still significant problems.

## Supply Chains – The UK Modern Slavery Act 2015

Since the UK's Modern Slavery Act (MSA) came into force it has been widely considered as a game-changer in fostering greater transparency among companies that had long been ignorant of human rights abuses happening along their supply chains.

The Transparency in Supply Chains provision states that all businesses with over £36m turnover must publish an annual slavery and human trafficking statement (on their website with a link from the homepage) stating what steps they have taken to ensure that there is no modern slavery in its business or global supply chains.

The statement should lay out steps that the business is taking to identify and remove any abusive practices from its supply chain and it must be approved by the Board, signed by a director, and placed in a prominent place on the business's website.

## Are companies that meet the threshold complying with disclosure obligations?

At the time of writing, many companies were starting to publish their second year statements and were beginning to recognise the geographical areas and hotspots within their companies with regard to forced labour and slavery. Companies realise that the key business objectives of tackling modern slavery include:

- protecting and enhancing an organisation's reputation and brand
- protecting and growing the organisation's customer base as more consumers seek out businesses with higher ethical standards
- improved investor confidence
- greater staff retention and loyalty based on values and respect
- developing more responsive, stable and innovative supply chains

In order to meet these objectives, certain companies are more vigorous in creating policies and procedures which will more strenuously identify and tackle forced labour and slavery at all levels in their supply chains. There is still much that needs to be done as the analysis and due diligence are also affected by financial constraints.

---

- Marks & Spencer has, as of May 2016, revised its "global sourcing principles" on forced labour and agency labour by adding a new statement prohibiting the payment of direct or indirect recruitment fees to secure a job, and requiring suppliers to have adequate due diligence in place to ensure this does not happen.
- Sky plc has conducted a specific modern slavery risk assessment across its own operations and all its suppliers.
- Burberry is developing specific modern slavery and labour rights training for key Burberry employees who interact with its supply chain networks.
- Lush cosmetics and Free the People are pushing for ethical integrity and key training.

Carrier P & Bardwell J in *Open Democracy,* 24 January 2017

---

## Fairtrade and equivalent organisations

Fairtrade is a social movement whose stated goal is to help producers in developing countries achieve better trading conditions and to promote sustainable farming. Members of the movement advocate the payment of higher prices to exporters, as well as improved social and environmental standards.

The movement focuses in particular on commodities, or products which are typically exported from developing countries to developed countries, but also consumed in domestic markets (for example Brazil, India and Bangladesh) most notably via handicrafts, coffee, cocoa, wine, sugar, fresh fruit, chocolate, flowers and gold.

There are several recognised fairtrade certifiers, including Fairtrade International (formerly called FLO, Fairtrade Labelling Organizations International), IMO Fair for Life and Small Producers' Symbol - each provide a certification on either a product or an organisation upon the basis of the commitment to the fairtrade principles.

The basis of the Fairtrade model does bring incredible benefits to communities – it ensures that the people who create fairtrade products enjoy a living wage that is often higher than they would typically earn and fairtrade cooperatives allow participants to invest and support education and medical care within a community.

Fairtrade workers are also ensured safe conditions of work and an equal platform is provided for all workers as discrimination based on factors such as religion and gender is banned in fairtrade businesses.

Child labour is also substantially reduced because workers earn fair wages and that lessens the need of families to make their children work to help support the household.

## The work of the churches

As with most social issues it is the churches and faith groups that have, in a significant way, led and participated in the fight against this social evil.

# The Catholic Church in England and Wales

"The Catholic Church intends to intervene in every phase of the trafficking of human beings: she wants to protect them from deception and solicitation; she wants to find them and free them when they are transported and reduced to slavery; she wants to assist them once they are freed. Often the people who are trapped and mistreated lose the ability to trust others, and the Church often proves to be the last lifeline.

It is absolutely essential to respond in a concrete way to the vulnerability of those who are at risk, so as to then guide the process of liberation beginning with saving their lives."

*Pope Francis, Address to participants in the World Day of Prayer, Reflection and Action against Human Trafficking, 12 February 2018*

The Medaille Trust was arguably the first to enter the UK field and the largest Catholic charity currently engaged in anti-trafficking work.

A variety of other Catholic charities within the UK is also working in this field and some of their work is shown below:

## The St Bakhita Initiative

There are three related projects to the initiative:

- The Santa Marta Group is an alliance of police chiefs and bishops from around the world, working together with civic society to counter human trafficking. Pope Francis, who has called human trafficking "an open wound on the body of contemporary society", endorses the process. Cardinal Vincent Nichols, Archbishop of Westminster, leads the Group, named after the Papal residence where the participants at the Vatican Conference stayed in April 2014. This resulted in a signed "Declaration of Commitment" by all the chiefs of police present to work together with the Church globally. http://santamartagroup.com

- The Bakhita Research Institute will focus on high-level applied research and international networking between the Church, Government, Civic Societies and law enforcement agencies. At present it is planned that a number of research strands will be followed:
  - the development and sharing of applied research on patterns of trafficking
  - the provision of materials for education, prevention and awareness-raising
  - the development of training programmes for professionals in the UK and internationally
  - the sharing of best practice for supporting those who have experienced human trafficking

Following a period of development the Institute will partner with St Mary's University, Twickenham.

- Managed by Caritas Westminster, Bakhita House in London provides assistance to female victims and possible victims of trafficking. It concentrates on working with the Metropolitan Police for those women who, for one reason or another, cannot or do not wish to enter the National Referral Mechanism. It provides an emergency placement for women escaping human trafficking and supports the beginning of the restorative process. Care comes in the form of
  - emergency support
  - medical and psychological therapy
  - legal and financial assistance
  - mentoring and help with accessing accommodation

Bakhita House is supported by the Adoratrice Sisters. https://thebakhitahouse.com

## Prevention and Protection

**Women at the well** is a female-only drop-in centre in Kings Cross, London dedicated to supporting women whose lives are affected by, or at risk of being affected by, prostitution. Most women who use the services have multiple and complex needs including:

- problematic drug and alcohol abuse
- mental health difficulties
- rough sleeping
- trafficking

The service opened in 2007 and is a project of the Institute of Our Lady of Mercy better known as the Sisters of Mercy. https://www.watw.org.uk

**Anawim** operates women's centres in Birmingham. The Hebrew Old Testament word "anawim" means "those who are bowed down". The word refers to poor people of every sort: those who are vulnerable, marginalised, oppressed and powerless. They depend totally on God for everything because they are otherwise without resources.

Anawim in Birmingham exists to help women over eighteen and their children to move their lives forward from their involvement in and surroundings of, prostitution, offending behaviour, drug abuse and sexual exploitation. It offers a variety of services both at the centres and by means of outreach including the provision of:

- courses and activities, skills, awareness and social responsibility
- counselling
- support with parenting, child protection, safeguarding and pregnancy
- drop-in facilities to access support, clothes, food and use of the phone and Internet
- advocacy services for women and their children with social care and health, education, work providers, the criminal justice system and the wider community
- assistance and support to women on the street at night, in prison, at court and in their workplace

Anawim was a joint project of Our Lady of Charity and Father Hudson's Society but became a registered charity in its own right in 2015. http://www.anawim.co.uk

**Rahab** is a charity founded by the Adoratrice Sisters in 2009 to care for women affected by prostitution and human trafficking for sexual exploitation.

The biblical Rahab was a prostitute who turned her life around and in so doing became someone who is remembered for her religious faith and good works.

The organisation which has adopted Rahab's name operates largely in London and seeks to be a "source of encouragement to the women – embracing a shared humanity, strengthening them through the struggles they face with love, compassion and understanding". It supports Bakhita House, has engaged in EU-funded anti-trafficking projects and operates street outreach and brothel visits, often with the police. http://www.rahabuk.com

**The Olallo Services** are a project of the Order of St John of God, named after "Blessed José Olallo Valdés, a Cuban Brother of the Hospitaller Order of Saint John of God, who dedicated his life to serving the sick, the wounded and dying on both sides in Cuba's first war of independence from Spain, and the victims of cholera".

The Olallo Project is based in central London. It offers advice, training, short-term and move-on accommodation to support people, including migrants, who are homeless, with no recourse to public funds, in order that they are able to find a place in society, or return to their country of origin. As part of their mission they have begun to offer support and accommodation to victims of trafficking. https://sjogfoundation.ie/uk/olallo-house

**The Arise Foundation** is a charity based in London and New York, founded on the belief that more should be done to support grass-roots anti-slavery networks. Its mission is to help these networks reach their potential by providing the support they need whether that is financial, digital, administrative or capacity-building in its nature. They work to raise awareness, promote respect for dignity, provide shelter and care and obtain justice. https://arise.foundation

**Trafficking Awareness-Raising and Campaigning (TRAC)** is an initiative working to end sex trafficking, formed by representatives from Congregations of Religious Sisters in the UK. A significant number of Religious Congregations of Sisters from across the UK are represented at their meetings and the membership provides links to many networks and organisations – Unanima, Renate, UISG and Talitha Kum are examples.

TRAC has produced basic information leaflets which are updated regularly, leaflets for prison governors and chaplains, a speaker's pack including information, resources, prayer material and handouts, prayer cards and prayer materials, *The Way of the Cross* (available also on DVD) and PowerPoint presentations used for awareness-raising with different groups. TRAC give talks and workshops to schools, parish groups, diocesan meetings, Justice and Peace conferences, Religious Congregations and faith-based groups, clubs and societies.

TRAC's aim is to keep a wide audience up to date with the latest developments such as EU directives, the latest UK strategies, UK & European human trafficking reports, UK legislation and Catholic social teaching.

It is currently particularly focused on looking at ways to address the issue of demand and the issue of grooming and domestic trafficking within the UK. It is an advocate for the Nordic Model.

Through theological reflections, TRAC brings a faith perspective and a prayerful discernment to its work that help to enrich and focus engagement with the issues.

TRAC was originally formed in 2006 by representatives of many of the founding member Congregations of the Medaille Trust. These were Sisters who wished to work to educate, raise awareness and campaign on the issue of human trafficking. TRAC is now an independent organisation. https://www.traconline.org.uk

As can be seen the effort of the Catholic Church in the UK is significant, particularly because it also has international relationships and partnerships with a variety of other Catholic organisations involved in the fight against trafficking and slavery, such as Renate in Europe and Talitha Kum worldwide.

## Other faith responses

Of course the Catholic Church is not the only faith group involved in the fight although it has, arguably, done the most.

A particular initiative that may prove of great benefit in future years has just begun at the time of writing.

The Church of England's Clewer Initiative (https://www.theclewerinitiative.org) is a three-year project to enable Church of England Dioceses and wider church networks to develop strategies to detect modern slavery in their communities and help provide victim support and care.

It involves working locally with Anglican parishes, identifying resources that can be utilised, developing partnerships with others, and creating a wider network of advocates seeking to end modern slavery through working in partnership.

Nationally, it involves developing a network of practitioners committed to sharing models of best practice and providing evidence-based data to resource the Anglican national engagement with statutory and non-statutory bodies.

The initiative forms part of the Church of England's approach to eradicating modern slavery and is funded by the Clewer Sisters. They are Anglican Augustinian nuns, founded in 1852 to help marginalised, mainly young women, who found themselves homeless and drawn into the sex trade, by providing them with shelter and teaching them a trade.

## Secular NGOs and partnerships

Of course the churches are not the only part of civil society engaged in the fight against trafficking and a range of secular NGOs has arisen in recent years to join the fight.

Stop The Traffik concentrates on raising awareness and mobilising community action. (https://www.stopthetraffik.org)

The Human Trafficking Foundation lobbies and campaigns for more Government action against trafficking and slavery. (https://www.humantraffickingfoundation.org)

The Sophie Hayes Foundation (https://sophiehayesfoundation.org) and Kalayaan (http://www.kalayaan.org.uk) provide services to victims.

The range of charities involved is large and diverse and offers a richness of differing approaches and thinking in the sector.

## How we can all be involved in the fight

It is hoped that this book will have prompted at least some readers to ask "what can I do?" or "how can I help?"   Listed below are some areas that those who wish to join the struggle may like to consider:

- Make a donation to a charity of your choice:
  - financial support is always appreciated
  - gifts in kind that will be useful, for example, bedding, toiletries or food to a safe house
  - gift your time by volunteering
- Spread awareness of the problem by talking to friends, family and colleagues about the issues.
- If you see anything suspicious, report it to the police.
- Consider how you can change your purchasing and consuming habits to avoid supporting industries and products that involve labour exploitation and slavery.
- Become an activist – set up or join a community group working against slavery, write to your MP and sign petitions.
- Pray for the victims, pray for staff who support them, pray for the efforts of law enforcement agencies and pray for the traffickers that their hearts may turn from this evil crime.

The fight against slavery is everyone's fight. It is far too important a subject to be left solely to the Government.

"Having few opportunities for regular channels [of migration], many immigrants decide to take alternative routes, where all manner of abuses, exploitation and slavery await them. Criminal organisations involved in human trafficking exploit these migration routes to hide their victims among the migrants and refugees. I thus invite everyone, citizens and institutions, to combine their efforts to prevent trafficking and guarantee protection and aid to the victims.

Let us all pray that the Lord may convert the hearts of traffickers — this is an ugly word; traffickers in human beings — and give those who are caught in this shameful scourge the realistic hope of regaining their freedom."

*Pope Francis, General Audience, 7 February 2018*

# FURTHER READING

There is a variety of books published on human trafficking and modern slavery. However, UK-focused books tend to be legal, academic or technical handbooks, interspersed with some sensationalist memoirs.

However, shown below are some works suggested as further reading for those wishing to further expand their knowledge. Most are available through Amazon.

- Bales K, Trodd Z, Williamson AK (2011) *Modern Slavery: A Beginner's Guide*
- Bales K (2012) *Disposable People: New Slavery in the Global Economy*
- Chalke S (2009) *Stop the Traffik: People shouldn't be bought and sold: The Crime That Shames Us All*
- Chandran P (Ed) (2011) *Human Trafficking Handbook: Recognising Trafficking and Modern-Day Slavery in the UK*
- Hayes S (2012) *Trafficked: The Terrifying True Story of a British Girl Forced into the Sex Trade*
- Kara S (2010) *Sex Trafficking: Inside the Business of Modern Slavery*
- Lee M (2007) *Human Trafficking*
- Muhsen Z (1994) *Sold: One woman's true account of modern slavery*
- Shelley L (2011) *Human Trafficking: A Global Perspective*
- US Department of State (2017) *Trafficking in Persons Report*
- Waugh L (2006) *Selling Olga*

If you would like to know more about the work of the Medaille Trust or you would like to book a talk with one of their Diocesan Representatives, please visit the website www.medaille.co.uk or email mtenquiries@medaille-trust.org.uk

# REFERENCES

Dirie W (1998) *Desert Flower*, New York, William Morrow.

Bales K and Soodalter R (2009) *The Slave Next Door*, California, University of California Press.

Glenny M (2008) *McMafia: A Journey Through the Criminal Underworld*, London: Penguin.

Hayes S (2012) *Trafficked: My Story*, London: Harper Collins.